Maximum Return, Minimum Risk: A Practical Approach

By James B. Cloonan, Ph.D.

American Association of Individual Investors
625 North Michigan Avenue
Chicago, Illinois 60611
(312) 280-0170; (800) 428-2244
www.aaii.com
ISBN: 1-883328-15-2   Rev-1

Preface

Over the years, a volume of literature has been written on investment risk, a large part of it extremely technical. While the concept of risk is fairly straightforward and most of us know what it means in many circumstances, it becomes much more complex when we try to quantify it.

Risk comes into play with the simplest of games—a coin toss, roulette, craps—where the odds are reasonably easy to determine and static. It becomes more complex with games like blackjack where the odds change as cards are played. In games like poker and bridge, the pure odds are changed with knowledge of the previous behavior of opponents. However, all of these are simple compared to the multi-faceted probabilities of real-world investing.

Investment risk and its measurement are complex because the risk we take will occur in a future we cannot know. Using past experience, however, we can make estimates both by analytic means and common sense that will give us some understanding of and control over the risk of our portfolios. Attaining that degree of understanding and control is the purpose of this book.

While many of the concepts I discuss here have a mathematical foundation, I have tried to keep the math out of the main body of the analysis for clarity. The statistical underpinnings are important, however, and are presented in Appendix A. The notations A1, A2, etc., indicate mathematical explanations that are found in

Appendix A. In addition to the equations in Appendix A, we also present an explanation and, where possible, an easy way to perform computerized analysis using an Excel spreadsheet program.

Individual stock selection is not discussed in this book. While risk control involves making some choices in the methods used in selecting asset classes and individual stocks, the approaches to risk control in this book assume you have chosen a strategy for selecting individual assets, whether by your own analysis or using another's methods.

I thank the AAII analytic and editorial staffs for all of their help in the preparation of this book. The content, analysis, and any errors herein are my own and reflect my own biases and opinions. There are many who would disagree with me, and there are other approaches for the control of risk not covered here that other analysts would consider important.

I have made considerable effort to keep this book short and understandable. It is my hope that the contents of this book will prove helpful on a day-to-day basis as you try to balance the desire to obtain maximum return on your portfolio with the need to control the riskiness of your assets.

James B. Cloonan, Ph.D.
June 30, 2003
Chicago, Illinois

Table of Contents

Introduction

"If I pick good stocks why should I be concerned with risk?" This is a question asked by many individual investors either out loud or to themselves. Most investors don't want to think about risk—sometimes for psychological reasons, sometimes because they don't understand it, and sometimes because the main focus of all the publications they read is on stock selection. Sure, risk is mentioned, but only in a lip-service way. It is rare indeed to find risk-adjusted returns for stocks, advisory portfolios, or mutual funds.

You may think: "If a mutual fund goes up 15%, then it went up 15%, what difference does the risk-adjusted rate of return make? None!" None in the past—but risk has a way of coming home to roost.

Basic Principle I

Reduction in portfolio risk can be directly converted into increased return. There is no easier way to increase the return on a portfolio than to reduce its unnecessary risk.

Basic Principle 2

Any individual security should be selected not because it has the highest ratio of expected return to risk over your investment horizon, but rather because it increases the return-to-risk ratio of your entire portfolio more than any other security choice.

The concept of risk goes beyond sleeping well: Risk and return are bound together as shown in the box on the previous page.

The first principle emphasizes the close connection between risk and return. That relationship goes beyond the basic concept that higher expected returns carry the burden of higher risk. The second principle is based on a belief in the *portfolio view*—the emphasis is on building and evaluating your entire portfolio of assets simultaneously, not on an asset-by-asset basis. As this book will show, your portfolio is, indeed, more than the sum of its parts.

Chapter 1 defines risk and focuses on its measurement. The next two chapters examine ways to reduce risk—diversification and asset allocation. Chapter 4 summarizes the relationship between risk and return. Following Chapter 4 is a special section for those who are using AAII's *Stock Superstars Report*.

There is another approch to risk reduction not addressed here—hedging. Hedging reduces overall risk by being short, or the equivalent, some portion of the portfolio. The most common approaches involve options, which alone require a thick volume (see Bibiography). In addition, the basic concept of hedging is very different from the approaches discussed in this book and needs extensive separate treatment.

The entire book provides the theoretical underpinnings of risk analysis, while focusing on practical ways to increase your investment success through risk control.

Chapter

Understanding Risk and How It Is Measured

Individuals invest in different assets in order to receive a return (a profit). Investors may have received this return in the past and expect to receive it in the future. But how dependable is the expected return? Enter the concept of risk.

Risk in general is defined as "the chance of damage, injury, or loss." Investment risk is the chance of loss, but it's not hard to also imagine cases of damage or injury to an investor's well-being as a result of taking on risk. To assess the chance of loss in an investment, it's necessary to refine the definition of risk and try to put it in mathematical terms.

Measuring Risk

Virtually all acceptable measures of risk are based on gauging the dependability of return on an investment. How is dependability measured? Investors look at the volatility of the returns— how much the returns of a security or portfolio vary around the average return. For example, consider two assets A and B as shown in Table 1.1 on page 5.

While the four-year arithmetic average return

for both investments is the same, 10%, you would have more money if you invested in Asset A. The terminal wealth would be $1.46 for every dollar invested as opposed to $1.43 with Asset B, or 2% more. The greater the variation around the arithmetic average return, the more the geometric average will be below the arithmetic average. And terminal wealth is determined by the geometric average. The geometric average is reduced relative to the arithmetic average as a function of volatility. (See A1 in Appendix A for the mathematical formula for geometric average.)

You can see this phenomenon quite easily by considering this situation: If you gain 20% and then lose 20%, you are not even but have lost 4%; if you gain 40% and then lose 40%, you are out 16%. The higher the variation, the more the terminal loss.

Table 1.1 also shows standard deviation, which is the most common measure of return volatility. Standard deviation is calculated as the square root of the average of the deviations from the average, squared (see A2 in Appendix A for the formula).

Why is this calculation used? Simply averaging the deviations from the average would result in some negative numbers and an average difficult to interpret. Looking at the range of returns— simply taking the difference between the two extremes (−0.05 − 0.25= −0.30, or 0.30)—would not show how tightly other returns were clustered. For example, consider the following two series of returns: −20.0, 0.0, 0.0, 0.0, +20.0 and −20.0, −19.0, 0.0, +19.0, +20.0. They each have the same range, but not the same volatility.

The first series of returns will have 4% higher terminal wealth.

Another measure of volatility that is quite direct is to look at a series of returns and observe the lowest cumulative return over the period under observation. This is called maximum drawdown and is a very common measure in commodities trading. Basically it measures the lowest level an equity reached during a specific period. As with all historical risk measures, maximum drawdown is presumed to be an indication of future risk. It's a useful measure no matter what risk measure is used, but because the drawdown in the future may be greater than in the past, maximum drawdown must be estimated and therefore becomes "expected" maximum

Table 1.1: The Impact of Volatility on Terminal Wealth

	Period Returns (%) 1	2	3	4	Arithmetic Average (%)	Standard Deviation (%)	Geometric Average (%)	$1 Invested: Terminal Wealth ($)
Portfolio A	10.0	10.0	10.0	10.0	10.0	0.00	10.0	1.46
Portfolio B	25.0	−5.0	5.0	15.0	10.0	11.20	9.4	1.43

Calculating the Averages:

Portfolio A
Arithmetic Average: [0.10 + 0.10 + 0.10 + 0.10] ÷ 4 = 0.10 = 10.0%
Geometric Average*: [(1 + 0.10) × (1 + 0.10) × (1 + 0.10) × (1 + 0.10)]$^{1/4}$ − 1.0 = 0.10 = 10.0%
Terminal Wealth of $1: $1 × [(1 + 0.10) × (1 + 0.10) × (1 + 0.10) × (1 + 0.10)] = $1.46

Portfolio B
Arithmetic Average: [0.25 − 0.05 + 0.05 + 0.15] ÷ 4 = 0.10 =10.0%
Geometric Average*: [(1 + 0.25) × (1 − 0.05) × (1 + 0.05) × (1 + 0.15)]$^{1/4}$ − 1.0 = 0.094 = 9.4%
Terminal Wealth of $1: $1 × [1 + 0.25) × (1 − 0.05) × (1 + 0.05) × (1 + 0.15)] = $1.43

* The Geometric Average takes into consideration the compounding effect of the prior period return earning money over the next period. In the equation, ¼ represents the fourth root of the amount in brackets. The fourth root of a number is the amount which, when multiplied by itself four times, results in that number [for example, if $N^{1/4} = R$, then $R \times R \times R \times R = N$].

5

loss. (The term "expected" is used to mean the best estimate of future return or future risk.) The weakness of historical drawdown is that there is nothing in the measure to indicate the probability of receiving the historical loss, or a greater loss, in the future.

Beta is a very common measure of risk, but it too has its drawbacks. Beta measures the risk of individual assets or portfolios relative to the risk of the stock market as a whole (see A7 in the Appendix for the formula). Market risk is also called systematic risk; it is the volatility all securities face and so it cannot be diversified away. (The volatility due to a security's unique characteristics is unsystematic risk, which can be reduced by combining the security with other dissimilar securities.) Beta is simply a measure of how much an asset's returns vary with the variation in the market's returns. Stocks with betas above 1.0 have returns that vary more than the market (have higher systematic risk) and those with returns that vary less than the market have betas of less than 1.0 (have lower systematic risk).

Beta is used less and less because the correlation between stocks seems to be decreasing, making beta less reliable. In addition, the proportion of stock risk that is systematic seems to be lessening over time. The validity of beta also depends on efficient market assumptions that are questionable. Finally, it is difficult to establish what a meaningful measure of the total market would be. The S&P 500, which is usually used, is really not representative of the entire market—nor is it relevant to the way most individuals invest.

Return Distributions

Standard deviation measures volatility on the upside as well as the downside. Clearly, investors don't worry much about their returns being volatile on the upside, although there is an advantage to having some consistency even among positive returns. If the distribution of returns is similar on the upside and downside, both positive and negative returns can be used in estimating volatility. However, examination of historical data shows that the distribution of investment gains and losses is not symmetrical—rather it tends to be stretched out more on one side. This is called skewness and is illustrated in Figure 1.1 (and also discussed further at A3 in Appendix A). Common sense explains the skewness: Losses can only be 100% on the downside (without the use of leverage), but gains can be unlimited on the upside.

How do researchers account for skewness in distributions of investment returns? There has

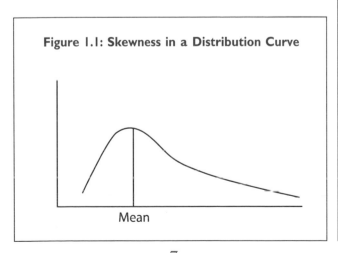

Figure 1.1: Skewness in a Distribution Curve

Mean

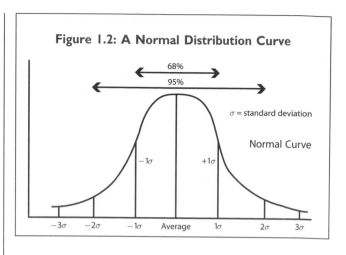

Figure 1.2: A Normal Distribution Curve

been some effort to cope with skewness directly by only measuring the dispersion below the average (see A6 on semi-variance in Appendix A). But the most common way of handling skewness is to ignore it on the basis that within the usual range of returns, skewness disappears. The lognormal curve, which is skewed, is a better estimate of the distribution of stock returns and is used in some models. But the regular normal curve is more commonly used and most estimates of probability you see are based on it. It is shown in Figure 1.2 (see A5 in Appendix A for further explanation of the normal curve).

Another problem with distributions of investment returns is that they tend to be more peaked and have longer tails (kurtosis) than a normal curve (see Figure 1.3 and A4 in Appendix A). While the great majority of observations of return are reasonably close to the average and do form close to a normal (or lognormal) distribution, the true distribution has a significant number of outliers (extreme values).

In fact, estimates of the true distribution of returns indicate the likelihood that the distribution has infinite variance and standard deviation. This means that the probabilities of loss indicated by the normal curve are not accurate and can be very misleading.

Again, since most of the return distribution is reasonably close to normal, these problems are ignored by most researchers. The assumption of normality in return distributions and the use of standard deviation as the basic measure of risk are almost universal in modern portfolio theory (MPT), which focuses on the relationship between risk and return to construct an optimal portfolio—one with the maximum return for a given level of risk. Further, these assumptions are not only used in assessing portfolio risk directly, but underlie most option evaluation models and the capital asset pricing model (CAPM)—an economic model for valuing stocks that relates risk to expected return.

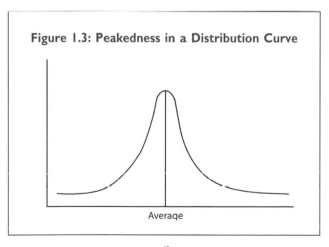

Figure 1.3: Peakedness in a Distribution Curve

Average

Though standard deviation and its variations will be used here, the problems with outliers should be kept in mind. Several times in an investment lifetime, market movements that could occur only once in a million years according to a normal curve will happen. Examples of this phenomenon occurred in 1929 and 1987. In fact, the frequent market moves of 3% a day during 2000–2002 should occur once a year at most, based on the assumption of a normal curve.

The failure of Long-Term Capital Management (LTCM), the hedge fund that made news in 1998, was due in large part to dismissal of outliers and an excessive use of leverage. LTCM was based on the many assumptions of modern portfolio theory, including the assumption of normalcy. The New York Federal Reserve was so concerned that the failure of LTCM would disrupt the U.S. economy that it took the unusual step of becoming involved in the problem and convinced a number of U.S. and foreign institutions to come up with $3.5 billion to save the fund. (The complete story is told by Roger Lowenstein in "When Genius Failed: The Rise and Fall of Long-Term Capital Management"; see Bibliography.)

How can investors use the strong analytic tools made possible by modern portfolio theory and not fall victim to outliers? There are several ways. The worst outlier problems occur with individual assets—even a large corporation's stock can go from incredible heights to near zero so quickly there is no chance to react. The solution here is diversification—a bit more diversification than might be called for under a normally distributed return assumption. Diversification will be covered in Chapter 2.

When the outliers relate to the market as a whole, asset protection is more difficult, but there are several actions that can be taken.

- First, keep a long-term view. While outliers might crush the short-term trader or even the one-year investor, outliers are much less likely to severely damage the returns of those with a three- to five-year horizon.

- Second, while investors can look at the probabilities indicated by the normal distribution in setting risk levels for themselves, this decision can be supplemented with analysis of what has happened historically over different horizons. Since 2001–2002 was one of the most sustained downturns in recent memory (at least in terms of major averages), investors can evaluate how they have coped and use this in setting risk levels in the future.

- Third, individuals can have some appropriate portion of their portfolio in assets or asset classes that have very low or negative correlations with the general stock market. This approach will be covered extensively in Chapter 3.

RiskGrades: Refining Standard Deviation

A variation of standard deviation called RiskGrades attempts to make standard deviation measures more meaningful. Developed by RiskMetrics Group, RiskGrades standardizes the somewhat meaningless levels of standard deviation by taking the average of all the world's equities during "normal" market movement periods between 1995 and 1999 and assigning it a standard deviation value of 100. All other standard deviations are expressed as a percentage of that figure. For example, a RiskGrade of 77 implies the portfolio or security has a risk 77% as high as the average risk of all equities in the world during normal market conditions. (For mathematical details of the approach, see the RiskGrades Web site link at www.aaii.com.)

There are a number of advantages to this variation on standard deviation:

• The risk of an asset or portfolio is related to the real world. The RiskGrade of an asset is approximately equal to five times its annual standard deviation.

• The result is converted to an annual value, even when the standard deviation or RiskGrade is calculated based on other periods—days, months, or quarters.

• RiskGrades can be calculated over any past period of time.

The volatility measurement tends to be fairly stable over the long term, but there is wide variation in the shorter term. Because asset adjustment may depend on current volatility, it is important to keep the measurement period short enough to pick up trends, but not so short that it

Figure 1.4: RiskGrades Chart Center— Six-Month Average RiskGrade

Source: RiskGrades.com by RiskMetrics Group.

picks up large fluctuations that are momentary. RiskGrades goes back in time but gives the most recent reading more weight. This provides a measure of volatility that is very sensitive to change. While the current RiskGrade is ideal for making comparisons between stocks, funds, and portfolios, it may be too volatile for making decisions about longer-term asset allocation. The six-month (or one-year) average RiskGrade can be used for that purpose (see Figure 1.4).

Most U.S. stocks have long-term annual RiskGrades of 50 to 500 (standard deviations of 10% to 100%). The S&P 500 has a long-term (40-year) RiskGrade of about 90. Risk in individual portfolios can be reduced below that of the average stock by diversification (covered in Chapter 2).

13

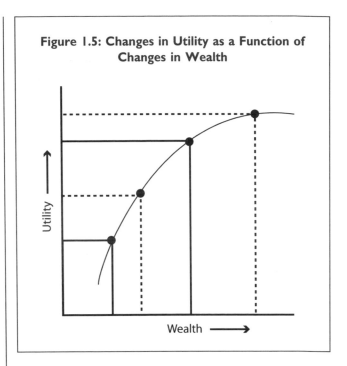

Figure 1.5: Changes in Utility as a Function of Changes in Wealth

Utility →

Wealth ⟶

Why Investors Are Risk Averse

It is reasonably easy to understand that obtaining successive amounts of additional money, while valuable, is not as valuable to an investor as holding on to what they already have. The general model for this diminishing marginal value of wealth is called utility theory and can be seen in Figure 1.5. Diminishing marginal utility simply means the next increment of wealth added is not worth as much to you as the previous increment.

This concept is particularly true in the area of investment risk and return. As an example, suppose someone offers to flip a fair coin with you. If you lose you must pay X dollars, but if you

14

win he will pay you 2X dollars. You think he is crazy and say OK, but then he says the bet is for most of your net worth. A 50% chance of losing all you have for a 50% chance to win twice your net worth is not a rational move for most individuals. You can measure your own decreasing marginal utility of money by following through on the process. Would you gamble two year's income, one year's, or one month's even at two-to-one odds on a 50-50 chance?

Because of decreasing marginal utility, investors are risk averse and are willing to sacrifice some potential return for reduced risk of loss. While this theory, developed by Daniel Bernoulli back in 1738, has been assumed to be true in general, if not in the precise logarithmic exposition, recent research indicates the theory does not explain real-world investor behavior. Investors may be "loss averse" rather than risk averse. That is, they may be willing to accept risk to avert loss, but not willing to accept risk for a gain. (Please see the Behavioral Finance section at the end of Chapter 4.) And the reduction of risk generally requires some reduction in return, as will be discussed in later chapters.

Chapter

Using Diversification to Control Risk

When discussing portfolio management, the concepts of asset allocation and diversification are often confused because diversification can be used in a general or specific way. *Diversification*, as we use it, is the choosing of assets within an asset class that are at least partially independent of each other in order to reduce risk. *Asset allocation* refers to the distribution of investment funds among distinct classes of assets. Asset allocation is not a goal, but rather an approach that attempts to achieve risk reduction, but doesn't always succeed. The ultimate goal of all investors, however, should be reducing risk to the level appropriate for them.

How Assets Are Grouped

Assets that have no long-term systematic movement with other assets can be considered a separate class. Chapter 1 introduced the concept of systematic risk, or volatility, as it applies to the stock market. Similarly, bonds and real estate also have their distinct forms of systematic risk.

However, there can be some correlation between asset classes from time to time. Correlation coefficients are used to measure how closely a pair of asset classes tends to move in relation to each other. A perfect positive correlation of 1.0 indicates the returns of both classes move up and down at the same time, but not necessarily by the same percentage. The less the correlation between classes, the better the opportunity for effective diversification. A negative correlation means that returns move together, but in opposite directions. Stocks and bonds have had correlations running from –0.3 to 0.6 over the past 70 years, but there is no systematic relationship. Real estate sometimes correlates with the stock market because a strong economy is good for both. Real estate also relates to the bond market because some real estate investments are influenced by interest rates. Basically, however, stocks, bonds (debt instruments), and real estate are the three primary asset classes.

What about assets that do not fit into these three groups? There are a wide range of commodities, including precious metals, that can be considered asset classes, but generally these are not assets that generate income. The only profit they generate is from price speculation (although it is often held that they can be effective hedges). However, the stock or bonds of gold mining companies are still stocks and bonds and belong in those asset classes, even though the movement of prices in precious metal mining stocks is correlated to the price of the metal as well as the other aspects of corporate success. But while investing in commodities, fine art, collectibles, etc., can be profitable and provide diversification for risk reduction, they are not included in the analysis in this book.

The view here is that the distribution of investments between the classes of stocks, bonds, and real estate is asset allocation. Subclasses of asset groups have emerged and are popular in the financial press. For stocks in particular, the subclasses of foreign vs. domestic, small cap vs. large cap, and value vs. growth have become part of the allocation process for some. This is not only a misleading but also an ineffective approach, as will be discussed more completely in Chapter 3.

Diversification Theory for Stocks

The modern portfolio theory (MPT) approach to diversification begins with the concepts of systematic and unsystematic risk. The very definition of systematic risk, risk resulting from general market action and not from the specific nature of the corporation or its stock, indicates that it cannot be diversified away. Figure 2.1 shows how diversification reduces the risk of a portfolio down toward the systematic (market) level.

Figure 2.1: Diversification and Risk

Standard Deviation of Portfolio

Unsystematic (Unique) Risk

Systematic (Market) Risk

Number of Stocks

While most stocks have systematic risk, they do not have the same degree of this risk. While systematic risk indicates that stocks move with the market, they do not all move to the same degree or even in the same direction. As described in Chapter 1, beta measures the systematic risk of a stock over a specified period. A beta of 1.0 indicates a stock whose returns vary to the same degree and direction that market returns vary. A beta of 1.5 indicates returns one and a half times as volatile as the market (if the market returns 10%, the stock returns 15% on average). A beta of 0.8 indicates that returns vary only 80% as much as the market. Beta can be negative, indicating a stock that moves with the market but in the opposite direction. A stock with a beta of –1.0 would have a return of –10%, on average, when the market returns 10%.

Since systematic risk is non-diversifiable, investors will want higher returns to justify accepting this risk. Figure 2.2 represents the security market line (SML), which indicates at a particular point in time what return can be expected for accepting a given level of market risk. Theoretically, in an efficient market all securities would lie on this line, but occasionally stocks appear outside the line, as shown by the two points representing stocks A and B. Clearly, stock A would be purchased before stocks on the SML because it provides a higher return for its level of risk. Just as clearly, stock B should not be purchased by any rational investor since its return is lower than its level of risk.

In an efficient market, stocks A and B will not stay above and below the SML for long. If

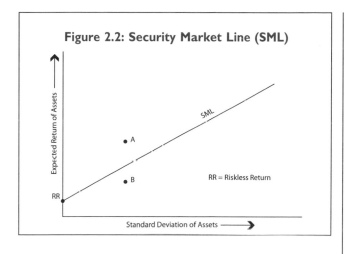

Figure 2.2: Security Market Line (SML)

Expected Return of Assets

SML

• A

• B

RR = Riskless Return

RR

Standard Deviation of Assets

everyone attempts to buy stock A, its price will be driven up (decreasing its expected return) until it resides on the SML. Similarly, stock B will be sold until its price goes down enough to raise its return to the level of the SML. It is important to note that even the least risky stocks may have a level of risk above that desired by an investor. In this case, to lower risk further the individual must go into another asset class.

In order to eliminate all the unsystematic risk (risk unique to the security), investors must diversify. Any approach to diversification recognizes that a number of stocks must be invested in, but the questions are: how many and which stocks? The naïve approach emphasizes obtaining diversification by increasing the number of stocks. But by simply adding stocks, the investor runs the risk of choosing ones that may have similarities (geography, industry, size) and thus would require more stocks than necessary to achieve an appropriate level of diversification.

21

Based on a large number of studies over the years, the following generalizations can be made:

1) Naïvely diversifying across industries will not provide better diversification than random diversification or choosing stocks without regard to their correlations. This does not preclude reducing risk by diversifying across industries if you choose industries in such a way as to reduce their correlations with each other.

2) Choosing a portfolio of stocks without regard to correlations will likely result in average correlations and a portfolio risk about 40% lower than the risk level of the average single stock. For example, if the average standard deviation of the stocks in your portfolio is 24%, you may be able to acheive a standard deviation of 14% in your portfolio. Most importantly, you can acheive this with about 15 stocks—additional stocks will not help noticeably.

3) Choosing stocks with low correlations to each other and the market can reduce the portfolio risk level even more—perhaps to less than 50% of the average standard deviation of the individual stocks in the portfolio. In this case, a slightly larger portfolio (20 to 30 stocks) will be worthwhile. You can estimate the standard deviation of a portfolio from the historical prices of the stocks in it (see formula A8 in Appendix A). But this formula is quite complex when more than a few stocks are involved.

4) It also appears inconclusive whether diversifying across capitalization size (large, mid, small) reduces risk. The same is true of diversifying across value and growth stocks. The correlation range within each of these subgroups is just as wide as between them. While such style diversification may reduce risk slightly, in a computerized world such a crude approach is like estimating people's weight from their height when there is a scale available. Measure portfolio risk directly, skip the simplistic approaches.

Computerizing the Theoretical Models

The concept of reducing portfolio risk by combining assets that are less than perfectly correlated is now well known. Since no perfect correlations are likely to be found among stocks, portfolios are always less risky than the individual stocks of which they are composed. Combining this with the expected (future estimated) returns of the stocks results in efficient portfolios—those with the maximum return for a given level of risk.

While such analysis was difficult years ago, modern computerized models make theoretical optimization possible. However, making precise estimates of the future returns of all stocks is not very accurate or feasible. In addition, many of the assumptions necessary in these analytic approaches are questionable. Beyond the problem of assuming a normal distribution of returns (discussed in Chapter 1), correlations are not consistent through time—adding significant error to statistical methods.

Modern portfolio theory is also hampered by its assumption that we have a highly efficient market. While the market appears to be reasonably efficient, it is not completely efficient for a number of reasons. First, assuming all investors used optimizing approaches in developing portfolios, they would not necessarily make the same estimates of the future risk and return of different equities. Thus, they might derive different valuations and choose different portfolios. Second, investors could all be using the same historical data, but the judgment as to how far back in time to go in making estimates would vary. Third, even if all information relating to every stock is known, the interpretation of this data may vary considerably.

As will be seen in Chapter 3, there are a number of well-established inefficiencies in the market that, together with the problems indicated in Chapter 1, have encouraged researchers to seek market models other than those based on previous modern portfolio theory. Newer models relieve some of the problems, but create problems of their own and so do not help with the goal here of reducing risk through diversification.

While the theoretical work accomplished through the years helps guide investors in the right direction, more practical ways of controlling risk need to be pinpointed. Interestingly, the Nobel Prize was recently awarded for work showing that the assumption of consistent rationality in investors is not always valid, and that markets often are inefficient. Additional studies show that humans depart from the assumed rationality and that "risk averse" may really be "loss averse." For example, an investor might refuse to buy a high-risk stock even with an opportunity for gain. But the same investor will hang on to this stock if he already owns it and take the same risk in order to avoid a loss. (See Kahneman in the Bibliography.)

Low Correlation Is the Key

Any practical attempt at risk reduction through diversification should start with the selection of stocks that are believed to offer superior returns. The various stock-picking approaches that have appeared over the years are not covered here. But the key when using any approach is to avoid choosing stocks whose returns will move together. While, as discussed earlier, random diversification across industries does not provide any more risk reduction than simple diversification, stock-picking approaches that result in choosing most stocks from similar industries will dampen any diversification effect.

One approach you can use with any selection strategy is to simply choose more stocks than you will eventually want. For example, if you want 20 stocks in your portfolio, select 30 to 40 stocks that you think may provide superior returns. Then reduce the number by keeping primarily the stocks with low correlations to the rest of the portfolio.

How do you check stock correlations? One method is to use a spreadsheet such as Excel that contains a correlation function. You can download historical data into the spreadsheet and set up a correlation matrix, as described in

Figure 2.3: RiskGrades: 10-Stock Portfolio

| Select Portfolio :
firstbooktest ▼ | Select Currency:
USD ▼ | CREATE NEW PORTFOLIO | CUSTOMIZE COLUMNS | |

firstbooktest   Set as default ○

- This portfolio's RiskGrade™ of 137 suggests _Speculative Plan investment strategy_.
- Diversification benefits have lowered this portfolio's risk by 41%.
- This portfolio is 1.01 times as volatile as the S&P - S&P 500 Index.

Portfolio Views ☑ EC ⊞ RA ▥ GV ☰ FA ⚠ RR ✏ PR

Symbol	Risk Grade™	Risk Impact	XLoss	XLoss %	% of Holding	Market Value	Risk Chart™
ACS	284	13%	$522	8.71%	11.32%	$5,999	☑
AMSG	231	5%	$227	6.59%	6.51%	$3,449	☑
COLM	212	15%	$373	4.93%	14.27%	$7,566	☑
DHI	277	10%	$285	7.37%	7.30%	$3,872	☑
LTD	281	11%	$272	6.61%	7.75%	$4,108	☑
MSA	205	3%	$177	5.08%	6.59%	$3,492	☑
NVR	232	11%	$322	5.78%	10.53%	$5,580	☑
RCI	129	4%	$180	2.98%	11.40%	$6,043	☑
STTX	282	5%	$418	5.92%	13.30%	$7,050	☑
WWW	215	13%	$332	5.67%	11.04%	$5,855	☑
Equities	137	100%	$1,631	3.00%	100.00%	$53,015	
Portfolio	137		$1,631	3.08%		$53,015	☑
Diversification Benefit	96		$1,478	47.54%			

Source: RiskGrades.com by RiskMetrics Group.

Appendix A under standard deviation (A2). After running the correlation function for all pairs of stocks, you can then choose the low correlation stocks visually. Not only can you vary the stocks selected but you can also weight the stocks with low correlations more heavily (invest more dollars in them). There is simulation software that will search for the lowest risk combination, but given other assumptions this is not really necessary.

Another method for picking low correlation stocks is provided at the RiskGrades Web site (introduced in Chapter 1). As suggested, choose more stocks than will eventually be needed and then go to the RiskGrades tool at AAII.com and enter these stocks in a portfolio (in the My Portfolio section). RiskGrades, which is free to individuals, will analyze the portfolio, showing the average risk of the stocks in the portfolio and the risk of the portfolio itself. The lower risk of the portfolio is the reduction due to diversification. The risk impact of each stock is also indicated, enabling you to see which stocks can be eliminated without increasing risk significantly. Various combinations can be tested until you reach a portfolio of the size you want.

You can see how this can be accomplished in Figures 2.3 and 2.4. If you were checking out 10 stocks that you liked but only wanted to have a portfolio of six stocks, you could do the following:

Put the 10 candidates into a RiskGrade portfolio (which results in the output shown in Figure 2.3). The four stocks with the highest risk impact are ACS, COLM, NVR, and WWW. In the event of a tie (as with NVR and LTD),

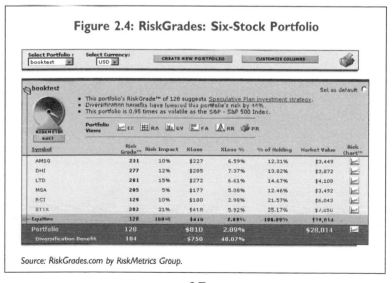

Figure 2.4: RiskGrades: Six-Stock Portfolio

Source: RiskGrades.com by RiskMetrics Group.

secondary criteria can be used to select one. Using the Edit function, eliminate those four stocks. When you click Save, you get the results in Figure 2.4.

Notice the risk of this six-stock portfolio is actually lower, 128, than the original 10-stock portfolio, 137. This is because it is more diversification efficient. The diversification benefit is 104 in Figure 2.4 versus 96 in Figure 2.3. This is an example of how adding more stocks not only doesn't reduce risk, it actually adds to it.

The weights of stocks can be changed, rather than investing equally in each one. Increasing the weights of the stocks contributing the least risk will provide the RiskGrade with the greatest reduction in risk from diversification. Keep in mind, however, that the RiskGrade given on the primary analysis section of the site is heavily weighted toward the volatility of the last two weeks. While this is fine for making comparisons between assets or portfolios, the six-month (or one-year) average RiskGrade is preferred for making asset allocation decisions (see Figure 1.4 in Chapter 1).

Chapter 3 reveals practical approaches to putting together a diversified portfolio in conjunction with allocating assets across classes and subclasses.

Combining Stock-Picking Approaches

Instead of selecting a larger number of stocks than is needed and then reducing portfolio risk by choosing the ones with low correlation, an

MAXIMUM RETURN, MINIMUM RISK: A PRACTICAL APPROACH

alternative is to combine several different stock-picking strategies or several different advisors' approaches. In either case, the important thing is to make sure the approaches are not essentially the same.

While diversification is generally based on past history on the theory that the relationships that existed in the past will continue to exist in the future, choosing stocks based on different criteria and fundamental approaches will almost guarantee diversification in the future. But the stock selections from different advisors or from different approaches can be checked by analysis using the RiskGrade procedure described above.

AAII uses the combination approach in its new *Stock Superstars Report* (*SSR*) advisory service. The starting point for the creation of the *Stock Superstars Report* concept was investment professionals whose approaches have beaten the market over very long time periods. The *Stock Superstars Report* builds on the work of well-known investors such as Benjamin Graham, William O'Neil, Peter Lynch, John Neff, Martin Zweig, Warren Buffett, David Dremen, John Templeton and others to develop a complete portfolio management system. The system includes monitoring the success of each approach in the current market and utilizing the four approaches that are working best. Risk reduction within the *SSR* portfolio has been significant and portfolios selected this way have been shown to have lower risk than the market. For more information on the *Stock Superstars Report* system, visit the Web site at www.stocksuperstars.com.

Diversifying Within the Real Estate Asset Group

The other major asset classes, bonds and real estate, also require diversification. In the case of real estate, the ability to diversify effectively with individual assets is severely limited. Individual real estate assets are extremely expensive and even partnership shares are generally limited to qualified investors (high net worth or income) who invest over $100,000. Even with several million dollars, diversification across different types of real estate and different geographical regions would be difficult.

One solution is to invest in REITs (real estate investment trusts). REITs are very similar to mutual funds except they invest in real estate enterprises, primarily the ownership, renting and managing of properties. Investors can find REITs involved in every area of real estate. The major subclasses of equity REITs, and their percentage of all equity REITs, are:

- Industrial/Office 33%,

- Residential 21%,

- Retail 20%,

- Diversified 9%,

- Lodging/Resort 6%, and

- Other 11%.

Mortgage REITs are closer to debt instruments

than real estate and should be considered part of the bond asset class.

REITs cannot invest in short-term speculation or development. Individuals who choose to invest in these aggressive areas must do so through a limited partnership, which would not have the mutual fund characteristics of a REIT. Every limited partnership is unique and without continuous pricing, correlations cannot be made with other real estate investments or with other asset classes.

Information about REITs, including performance data, can be found at the Reis (www.reis.com) and NAREIT (www.nareit.com) Web sites (see References). REITs can be analyzed for diversification in the same way as stocks by performing your own correlation analysis or using the RiskGrades Web site.

Another way to diversify is to purchase one of the mutual funds that invest in a wide range of REITs. The Vanguard REIT Index fund (VGSIX) is one example, and it is used in Chapter 3 as a stand-in for the REIT asset class. Other fund families also have REIT mutual funds. The Vanguard REIT Index fund is based on the Morgan Stanley REIT index and is capitalization-weighted. Although REITs are not evaluated here in terms of market capitalization (share price times number of shares outstanding), the comments about indexes in Chapter 3 might well apply. In any event, investors will need a method of choosing the best REITs, before looking at correlations, when selecting the REITs themselves.

Diversifying Within the Bond Asset Group

For the purposes of this book, the bond asset group includes all debt instruments, bonds, bank accounts, CDs, money market funds, etc.

Although the terms systematic and unsystematic risk are not used when discussing bonds, they do have diversifiable and non-diversifiable risk. The risk that is common to the entire bond market is interest rate risk. All bonds are affected by interest rate changes and generally in the same direction. However, as with stocks, not all bonds will be affected to the same degree. Generally, the longer the maturity date or the higher the duration (an alternate bond maturity measure that considers the present value of remaining payments, not just time), the greater will be the impact of an interest rate change. However, inflation and expected interest rate changes can alter the impact.

Since longer maturities usually provide both higher returns and greater risk within the same default risk segment, the normal economic risk/return pattern of rewarding greater non-diversifiable risk applies to bonds. It is possible to diversify across maturities: Building a portfolio with a range of maturity dates is called creating a ladder. The main use of investment-grade bonds should be controlling risk in a portfolio made up largely of higher return assets. Under this scenario, there is little reason to own anything but short-term bonds. However, there are certainly exceptions: Individuals may want to eliminate virtually all risk, or they may be satisfied with the returns they can receive from bonds and don't want to bother with the effort required to increase their returns.

The above does not apply to individuals who invest in higher risk or junk bonds. The high-yield bond group is a completely different area of investing; in many ways it is similar to investing in stocks since corporate profits are an important aspect of analysis. The analysis is a little more specialized because firms with high-yield bonds are generally not profitable. With high-yield bonds, default risk becomes a major concern. This is the risk that you will not receive your principal or your promised interest.

There is some default risk in all bonds, except U.S. government bonds and bonds guaranteed by the government. It is because of default risk that diversification of bond holdings becomes desirable. Unfortunately, there is no historical data from which to derive correlation tables and thus diversification becomes naïve. The riskiness of bonds is not determined by ordinary statistical analysis of returns. Bonds have limited life and by the time volatility, beyond interest rate volatility, showed up it would be too late for action. Default risk in bonds is based on ratings given by four agencies (Duff & Phelps, Fitch, Moody's, and Standard & Poor's). And while there are eight to 13 rating categories, they can be reduced to three basic grades: investment grade, speculative, and default. In the case of municipal (tax-free) bonds, insurance is also available on many issues. Ratings are based on estimates of the issuer's ability to repay, which is based on financial strength.

Because bonds trade most efficiently (low

transaction costs) in large blocks, often $100,000, a great deal of diversification is not practical for the vast majority of individuals. Most investors will find using a mutual fund or investing in government bonds the most efficient way to diversify. Those who invest in speculative or default bonds must find a way to diversify that avoids the default risk that is tied to a single factor such as industry problems, changes in the law, or regulatory issues that might affect all of one's holdings simultaneously.

Diversification Increases Returns

Effective diversification is the first line of defense in controlling and reducing risk. And the reduction of risk not only protects us from investment disaster but, as will be shown in Chapter 4, allows us to increase our returns by minimizing the percentage of assets we will need in low-return, protective assets.

Chapter 3

Combining Diversification With Asset Allocation

Asset allocation became a popular investment topic in recent years based on a mistaken interpretation of a research study. A published work showed that over 90% of the *variation* in investment returns was associated with asset allocation. But those quoting the research reported that over 90% of returns are determined by asset allocation as opposed to individual asset selection. The study said nothing about the impact on the level of returns, but this misinterpretation spawned a flurry of articles and Web pages devoted to asset allocation strategies.

Asset Allocation Usually Ignores the Destination

While they all take the same general approach, common asset allocation approaches disagree strongly on the details. The general approach is to mandate that at a certain age, you should have a certain percentage of your wealth in each of stocks, bonds, cash, and sometimes other asset classes such as real estate. Often, they further divide each class into subclasses. For example, stocks might be divided into: large vs. small, domestic vs. foreign, or value vs. growth. The approaches will then briefly mention that this reduces risk, but there will be no analysis of how it does this or proof that it works. The emphasis will be on the debate over whether a 50-year-old should have 50%, 60%, or 70% in equities.

Most of these writings treat the topic as if asset allocation were an end in itself, rather than one possible tool in the creation of a portfolio that provides the highest return for a given level of risk. This is akin to arguing about the best road to take before you decide where it is you want to go.

Readers of a certain age will remember Adele Davis, the famous nutritionist. When she would lecture, invariably she would be asked something like, "Are tomatoes good for me?" Her response would be, "Which tomatoes, grown where?" Similarly, the response to a writer advocating a certain percentage in bonds vs. stocks should be "Which bonds, which stocks?"

Take a portfolio that is 70% invested in an S&P 500 index fund and 30% in a bond index fund, and calculate its risk. Invariably, you could find a different 100% stock portfolio that is less risky than the 70%/30% indexed portfolio, and you could also find a 100% bond portfolio that is more risky.

Allocation may be helpful, but the key to risk control is the selection of the individual assets in the portfolio. Diversification within asset classes is more important than the allocation between classes because asset allocation is used only to eliminate risk that cannot be reduced by diversification—and almost always at a reduction in the rate of return. Choose individual investments first, allocate weightings later.

More Problems With Traditional Allocation Approaches

In addition to this general problem of mistaken emphasis, there are some special problems with the usual approach to asset allocation. These include:

- Stocks and bonds sometimes move in the same direction, sometimes in opposite directions, and sometimes independently. Any allocation between them must adjust to this reality.

- Foreign stocks in a portfolio may reduce short-term risk, but this effect dissipates over a few years as economic conditions travel. And there is a significant return reduction for the temporary benefit.

- Pigeonholing all stocks into either value or growth doesn't make sense. Fifteen percent of all stocks are truly value stocks, 15% are truly growth stocks, and 70% are "something else." If you allocate between a value index fund and a growth index fund, you are primarily investing in "something else" stocks, which may not have the risk-reducing effect you want.

- In any approach to controlling risk, investment horizon and risk aversion should be important factors. The use of age as a surrogate for investment horizon is too simplified. Some people retire at 62, while

37

many others work into their 80s. Many individuals do not plan on using up all assets during retirement, but want to pass their wealth on to heirs. So the level of risk any investor should assume at any point in time depends on factors more complex than age.

- The allocation of wealth across stocks of different sizes as a method of controlling risk has its limitations. Typically, the size of a stock is measured in terms of market capitalization (share price times number of shares outstanding), and classified as micro, small, medium or large. Since over the long run micro-cap stocks outperform other stocks, particularly large caps, it may make more sense to look for portfolio diversification within the small-cap, micro-cap and perhaps mid-cap markets. For individuals who use mutual funds, there is a real danger of over-investing in large-capitalization stocks and of not being adequately diversified because most funds weight their holdings based on market capitalizations (the larger the company, the more of the stock in the index). An S&P 500 index fund will have 24% of its assets invested in the largest 10 stocks. Not only is this too much concentration, but the largest stocks often have high correlations. So, you may think you are getting diversification, but you aren't. While it may come as a surprise, the S&P 500 index is not a very well-diversified portfolio, nor are most indexes.

Allocation between certain asset classes can be a

tool to reduce risk. However, simplistic approaches should be set aside in order to look at all the factors that influence the risk of a portfolio. And, most importantly, the nature of the individual assets in each class must be considered before deciding on the allocation between classes.

As previously discussed, only stocks, bonds, and real estate can be considered unique asset classes for our purposes. For convenience, stocks can be divided into first-level subclasses by capitalization size and value versus growth. Bonds can be divided into short term (which includes bank accounts and CDs) and longer term. We use three years as the short-term limit.

Implementing the Popular Approach

Here's how the popular approach typically works. Table 3.1 presents a list of major asset classes and subclasses (using index funds and exchange-traded index funds [ETFs] as surrogates), with their long-term (10-year) average returns and their shorter-term (six-month) average risk level. The 10-year time period was chosen because most individuals have longer-term holding periods, and the 10-year returns are the best estimate of long-term future returns. The shorter period for risk measurement is shown because short-term volatility reduces long-term returns. The RiskGrade index is used as the measure of risk (see Chapter 1 for an explanation of RiskGrades).

Table 3.1 also shows what percentage of each asset class could be combined with Treasury bills

Table 3.1: Return of Asset Classes

Asset Class	Mutual Fund or ETF Surrogate (Ticker Symbol)	RiskGrade (Last 6 Mos)	10-Yr Avg Annual Return (%)	Portfolio RiskGrade of 58 Asset/T-Bill Ratio (%)*	Portfolio RiskGrade of 58 Asset/T-Bill Return (%)**
U.S. Total Stock Market	VTSMX	102	9.41	57/43	7.27
Foreign Stocks	VGTSX	91	4.32 (1)	64/36	4.36
Large-Cap Stocks	VFINX	108	9.97	54/46	7.43
REITs	VGSIX	62	10.11 (2)	94/6	9.77
Large-Cap Growth	VIGRX	104	10.09	56/44	7.60
Large-Cap Value	VIVAX	114	9.4	51/49	6.97
Small-Cap Growth	IWO	108	4.34 (3)	54/46	4.39
Small-Cap Value	IWN	92	11.34 (4)	63/37	8.79
Micro Cap	DFSCX	73	13.14	79/21	11.31
Total Bond Market	VBMFX	17	6.95	341/–241	13.00 (5)
Gold Stocks	VGPMX	88	1.99	66/34	2.82
Cash (T-Bills)	90-Day T-Bills	0 (6)	4.44	—	—

* Percentage invested in asset and percentage invested in T-bills to produce a portfolio with a RiskGrade of 58.
** Return from Asset/T-Bill Portfolio with a RiskGrade of 58.
(1) Used Lipper Foreign Fund category average since fund is not 10 years old.
(2) Used Wilshire REIT index average since fund is not 10 years old.
(3) Used Russell Small-Cap Growth index average since fund is not 10 years old.
(4) Used Russell Small-Cap Value index average since fund is not 10 years old.
(5) For a portfolio with a RiskGrade of 58, bonds are leveraged by borrowing at the risk-free rate and the portfolio return is increased.
(6) On a daily basis, T-bills have some risk, but assuming a 90-day holding period there is no risk. For those with no short-term cash needs, one-year T-bills could be used for a higher return.

Data as of June 30, 2003.

to achieve a certain level of risk, in this instance a RiskGrade of 58—which, at the time of this writing, was the current risk level of the widely touted allocation 60% stocks/40% bonds. For example, a portfolio consisting of 54% large-cap stocks and 46% Treasury bills would achieve a RiskGrade of 58. Table 3.2 looks at some sample asset allocations and provides each portfolio's RiskGrade and expected return (based on the long-term historical return). The first two examples are typical recommendations among the major asset classes, and the second two examples are typical recommendations that include subclasses.

How do these portfolios stack up? It is suggested that individuals use a portfolio benchmark that consists of the highest-returning asset class combined with Treasury bills to reduce the risk to their appropriate risk level. The highest-returning asset class in Table 3.1 is micro-cap stock, and the benchmark combination that achieves the desired RiskGrade of 58 is 79% micro-cap stocks and 21% Treasury bills, with a return of 11.31%—that's the benchmark. In this example, you should not consider allocations with

Table 3.2: Sample Asset Allocations		
Portfolio*	6-Month Average RiskGrade	Return** (%)
Portfolio 1: 60% Stocks/40% Bonds	58***	8.43
Portfolio 2: 80% Stocks/20% Bonds	80	8.92
Portfolio 3: see below	64	8.04
Portfolio 4: see below	61	7.50
Allocations	Portfolio 3	Portfolio 4
Large-Cap Growth	20.0%	20.0%
Large-Cap Value	20.0%	20.0%
Small-Cap Growth	12.5%	10.0%
Small-Cap Value	12.5%	10.0%
Bonds	25.0%	20.0%
Cash	10.0%	10.0%
Gold Stocks	0.0%	10.0%

*Surrogates used in this table are the same as those used in Table 3.1; for Portfolios 1 and 2, stocks are all U.S. stocks (represented by VTSMX) and bonds are all bonds (represented by VBMFX).
**Based on 10-year historical average annual return.
***RiskGrade of 58 used for normalization in Table 3.1.

Data as of June 30, 2003.

41

poorer results than this benchmark.

However, none of the suggested allocations in Table 3.2 match this benchmark. In fact, it's easy to see that allocations alone across the various subclasses of stocks do not provide much risk reduction. It is interesting that Portfolio 3 and Portfolio 4, which are common recommendations, are not as good as Portfolio 1 on a risk/return basis. The addition of gold stocks to Portfolio 3 (as in Portfolio 4) reduces risk and return proportionately.

The Alternative: Build From the Bottom

There is no question that allocation across asset classes may reduce risk but we don't know by how much until we know which investments in each class are involved. What we want is to add holdings to our portfolio that, in our estimation, have good prospects for superior returns and have low correlations with the other holdings. Which particular class those assets belong to is not the important issue.

A more effective approach to controlling risk is to start from the bottom and find investments with the potential for good returns, and then to choose a portfolio from among those investments. The objective, once again, is to get the highest return within an acceptable level of risk. To control risk (unless you have a very high risk tolerance), it will probably be necessary to have some assets that are not equities or are a very different form of equity, such as real estate investment trusts (REITs).

The RiskGrade service on AAII.com can be used to develop such a portfolio—the RiskGrade of a portfolio takes into consideration correlation, since a portfolio of low correlation stocks will have lower volatility and, therefore, a lower RiskGrade.

One example of a portfolio that uses this approach is AAII's Individual Investor's Shadow Stock Portfolio. This experimental small-stock portfolio diversifies away over 70% of the individual stock risk (see the Bibliography for more information on this portfolio). In AAII's *Stock Superstars Report* (introduced in Chapter 2), the final stock choice is based on which new recommended stock helps reduce portfolio risk the most.

Another weakness in the traditional asset allocation approach is that the returns and risk levels of the benchmarks are averages for asset classes (Tables 3.1 and Table 3.2). Well-chosen portfolios—portfolios in which the individual securities that are selected have good return prospects and low return correlations—will have much better return/risk ratios than portfolios with securities that are the average in each asset class.

In addition, the indexes and mutual funds used as asset class benchmarks consist of portfolios that are capitalization-weighted—a greater percentage of the portfolio is invested in companies with larger market capitalizations. As previously pointed out, smaller-cap stocks outperform larger-cap stocks, so the same index stocks and portfolios would perform better if equally weighted. In fact, an investor throwing darts at a sheet of listed stocks, selecting 30, and investing an equal amount in each one would have an incredibly good chance of beating the S&P 500 by a significant margin over the long run.

The Problem With Traditional Rebalancing

What about changing allocations over time? The traditional approach would be that if the accepted allocation was 60% stocks and 40% bonds and the stock market ran up, you would need to sell stocks and buy bonds to maintain the original percentage allocation. Once again, the problem here is that the approach is losing sight of the true objective—to control risk. Perhaps selling stocks and buying more bonds when the market goes up is a good idea sometimes. But, maybe not.

Imagine that the U.S. moves into a bull market after several years of weakness. The first year would likely be very strong for stocks, and conventional wisdom would dictate readjusting the stock/bond mix. But what if—and it is not unlikely—because stocks are moving up with some consistency, their risk is going down, and with the economy starting to perk up and the Fed doing its thing, bonds are becoming more volatile (risky)? This scenario may be unfolding as this is being written.

The alternative rebalancing approach is to maintain your given risk level. And to maintain the risk level you have chosen, you might find you should actually be buying stocks and selling bonds as stocks go up. With RiskGrades or other sources of volatility information, you can monitor the risk of your portfolio on a continual basis and make adjustments as needed.

One word of caution: Regardless of the approach to rebalancing, don't do it too often. Annually is more than enough. Not only are transaction costs and perhaps taxes involved, but there is strong evidence of short-term serial correlation. In other words, assets going up tend to keep going up—at least in the short term.

Once again, artificial percentages that hope to control risk are silly in the computerized age when risk can be dealt with directly and diversification can be obtained by adjusting the assets in the portfolio using correlations. As you can see, conventional asset allocation is an effort to achieve diversification by dividing the individual investments among various asset classes and subclasses in the hope, sometimes misguided, that a mix will achieve efficient diversification. On the other hand, diversification is the effort to divide our investments among individual securities that have low correlations with each other and thus reduce risk.

Fundamental Concepts to Risk Reduction

Before starting to design a portfolio that addresses your risk/return needs in a practical way, it is important to understand some major concepts that underlie any approach.

1. Volatility Affects Returns

The variability of the return on a portfolio's

assets, which is the accepted definition of risk, affects not only the "sleep well" aspects of the portfolio, but also the real return. This was pointed out at the beginning of Chapter 1 and is the result of volatility reducing the geometric return, which is the determinant of terminal wealth.

2. Diversification Affects Returns

While effective diversification will reduce risk, it may reduce return as well. This is because not all potential investments have the same likelihood of gain. If you didn't care about risk, you would put all of your assets into the single investment you thought had the likelihood of the greatest gain. But in order to diversify, you must put some assets in investments that you expect will have less potential return. At the same time, however, you anticipate that the reduced risk will be worth the reduced gain. Trying to reduce risk while giving up as little return as possible is the critical part of the strategy suggested in this book, which will be emphasized in Chapter 4.

3. Cap-Weighting Affects Returns

Although the risk and return data of the indexes of various asset classes is used as a surrogate for the risk and return of the various classes themselves, portfolios chosen by astute investors from these asset classes, as previously pointed out, should have higher returns and lower risk than the indexes themselves. On the other hand, if you use mutual funds instead of individual stocks, the risk and return may be closer to the indexes, since many mutual funds cap-weight their portfolios.

In addition, the larger capitalization stocks tend not to be value stocks, yet value stocks, as defined by their lower price-to-book ratios (stock price per share divided by book value per share), outperform growth stocks over the long run. As an example of this effect, over the last 10 years the Wilshire 5000 index has had an average annual return (through June 30, 2003) of 9.53%. However, the return of the Wilshire 5000 unweighted by market capitalization (in other words, the average stock in the Wilshire 5000) was 16.30% a year. This is the return the average dart thrower would have received on stocks. And to throw in another shocker: The Nasdaq composite index was down dramatically in 2002, with a return of –31.14%, yet the average stock on the Nasdaq was up 73.10%. The average stock has been up each year from 2000 to 2002—a period characterized as a bear market by most major stock indexes. You can monitor this difference at the Wilshire Web site at no charge (www.wilshire.com, click on Indexes, then Index Return Calculator). This is why the dart thrower should outperform the indexes and a thoughtful individual should outperform the dart thrower.

Note, too, that the risk in the weighted indexes is increased because the stocks that are most heavily weighted tend to be correlated, and thus diversification among these larger stocks has less impact. Small- and micro-cap indexes also are capitalization-weighted, and equally weighted individual stock portfolios chosen from these asset subclasses will have higher returns than the indexes. For example, on July 15, 2003, the diversification effect reduced risk by:

- 37% in the S&P 500,

- 31% in the Nasdaq composite,

- 71% in AAII's Individual Investor's Shadow
  Stock Portfolio, and

- 53% in AAII's *Stock Superstars Report*
  portfolio.

Table 3.3 shows correlations among the various indexes. Numbers approaching 1.0 indicate greater correlation in return performance; negative correlations indicate that returns tend to move inversely. When one index has a positive return, the other tends to be down. Whatever the risk and return levels of the indexes used, you can expect that your portfolio, if not cap-weighted, will have a lower risk and a higher return.

Table 3.3 Correlation of Asset

Asset Class	Total Stock Mkt	Foreign	Large Cap	REITs	Gold
Total Stock Market	—	0.88	0.99	0.28	0.35
Foreign	0.88	—	0.87	0.39	0.44
Large Cap	0.99	0.87	—	0.24	0.33
REITs	0.28	0.39	0.24	—	0.19
Gold	0.35	0.44	0.33	0.19	—
Large-Cap Growth	0.95	0.78	0.95	0.10	0.27
Large-Cap Value	0.94	0.88	0.95	0.38	0.35
Small-Cap Growth	0.88	0.81	0.83	0.27	0.39
Small-Cap Value	0.79	0.80	0.74	0.55	0.39
Total Bond Market	−0.34	−0.25	−0.36	−0.19	0.08
Short-Term Bond	−0.42	−0.37	−0.43	−0.23	0.03
Micro-Cap	0.85	0.78	0.80	0.40	0.36

Data as of June 30, 2003.

How can you develop a portfolio that establishes a risk level suitable for you and offers the highest returns while maintaining that level of risk?

There are two steps:

• Establish a level of risk you can live with, and

• Choose the individual assets and asset classes that will provide the highest return within that risk level. Table 3.3, along with Table 3.4, which shows asset class returns and volatility, can provide some guidance.

Setting a Suitable Risk Level for Yourself

There are a number of ways you can approach setting a suitable risk level. By looking at the standard deviation of returns for different classes

Classes (Based on Three-Year Returns)

Large-Cap Grth	Large-Cap Value	Small-Cap Grth	Small-Cap Value	Total Bond Mkt	Short-Term Bond	Micro-Cap	Index (Ticker)
0.95	0.94	0.88	0.79	−0.34	0.42	0.85	VTSMX
0.78	0.88	0.81	0.80	−0.25	−0.37	0.78	VGTSX
0.95	0.95	0.83	0.74	−0.36	−0.43	0.80	VFINX
0.10	0.38	0.27	0.55	−0.19	−0.23	0.40	VGSIX
0.27	0.35	0.39	0.39	0.08	0.03	0.36	VGPMX
—	0.81	0.77	0.60	−0.38	−0.45	0.74	VIGRX
0.81	—	0.79	0.82	−0.29	−0.36	0.79	VIVAX
0.77	0.79	—	0.87	−0.23	−0.35	0.85	VISGX
0.60	0.82	0.87	—	−0.14	−0.25	0.86	VISVX
−0.38	−0.29	−0.23	−0.14	—	0.94	−0.19	VBMFX
−0.45	−0.36	−0.35	−0.25	0.94	—	−0.28	VBISX
0.74	0.79	0.85	0.86	−0.19	−0.28	—	DFSCX

Table 3.4: Asset Class Return and Volatility

Asset Class	Index	Ticker
U.S. Total Stock Market	Vanguard Total Stock	VTSMX
Foreign Stocks	Vanguard Total International Stock	VGTSX
Large-Cap Stocks	Vanguard 500 Index	VFINX
REITs	Vanguard REIT Index	VGSIX
Gold	Vanguard Precious Metals	VGPMX
Large-Cap Growth	Vanguard Growth Index	VIGRX
Large-Cap Value	Vanguard Value Index	VIVAX
Small-Cap Growth	Vanguard Small-Cap Growth Index	VISGX
Small-Cap Value	Vanguard Small-Cap Value Index	VISVX
Total Bond Market	Vanguard Total Bond Index	VBMFX
Short-Term Bond	Vanguard Short-Term Bond Index	VBISX
Micro-Cap	DFS U.S. Micro Cap	DFSCX

(1) Used Lipper Foreign Fund category average since fund is not 10 years old.
(2) Used Wilshire REIT index average since fund is not 10 years old.
(3) Used Russell Small-Cap Growth index average since fund is not 10 years old.
(4) Used Russell Small-Cap Value index average since fund is not 10 years old.
(5) Used Lipper Short-Term Bond Fund category average since fund is not 10 years old.

Data as of June 30, 2003.

and using the normal curve, you can establish the percentage chance of losing different portions of your assets during a particular time period. Those probabilities can be seen in the Appendix A discussion of the normal curve (A5). [A similar approach, in the context of mutual fund investing, was described in an article that originally appeared in the *AAII Journal* and is reprinted in Appendix B.] However, there is a shorter approach that is more intuitive and avoids the problem of outliers when using a normal curve for the distribution of investment returns (as explained in Chapter 1).

The first assumption is that you are a long-term investor: If your holding period is less than three years, you should not be in stocks, but in low-risk debt instruments. Examining the history of the stock market since World War II can help you

3-Yr Avg Annual Return (%)	Standard Deviation (%)	10-Yr Avg Annual Return (%)
−10.58	17.55	9.41
−13.04	15.73	4.32 (1)
−11.26	16.90	9.97
13.80	14.11	10.11 (2)
23.64	35.43	1.99
−17.71	17.13	10.09
−4.34	18.70	9.41
−3.75	22.55	4.34 (3)
7.50	24.12	11.34 (4)
9.34	3.42	6.95
7.90	2.24	5.46 (5)
4.27	25.83	13.14

judge your reaction to losing periods. Since 1946, what is the worst that could have happened to your portfolio if all you held was the S&P 500 index?

During the 1973–74 period (based on calendar years), you would have lost 37.4% of your investment in the S&P 500. The three-year period of 2000–2002 had a loss of approximately 43%. In both cases, the loss indicated is based on buying at the top. This is generally not the case since investors usually buy stocks over time and the actual loss would be less or no real loss at all. But people tend to look at the highest level their portolio reached and measure loss from that point—at least from the highest year end.

For the purposes of this book, the recent down period is of benefit. When discussing risk in past periods, investors tend to say they would have ridden it through because they know it turned out all right. But the S&P 500 could go down again. Did you ride through this downturn or did you reduce your equity holdings, indicating your portfolio risk was inappropriately high? Nothing will give you more guidance about your risk tolerance level than an honest appraisal of your feelings and portfolio actions during the 2000–2002 period.

Assume the S&P 500 will have several periods of a 40% drop during your investment lifetime. The S&P has a long-term standard deviation of 18%, and a RiskGrade of 90, so this should provide an indication of what standard deviation or RiskGrade you are willing to assume. Contemplating occasional losses in the range of 40% and knowing how you felt during this past year should enable you to set an appropriate risk level. For example:

- If you can face a roughly 40% drop every 25 to 30 years and believe that in the long run stocks will prosper, you don't need to be in any asset class outside of U.S. stocks, although you will still want to diversify to keep your risk as low as possible while obtaining the long-term high return of stocks. (This does not include your short-term cash reserves as part of your investment portfolio.)

- If, on the other hand, you can only face a maximum of a 20% loss, you will need a portfolio with a standard deviation of about 9%, or a RiskGrade of 45. It will be difficult to reduce risk much below this level without moving out of stocks almost completely.

Assume for this discussion that you want to keep portfolio decreases below 30%, which implies a portfolio standard deviation of below 13.5%, or a RiskGrade below 67.5. You may recall from the earlier discussion and Tables 3.1

52

and 3.2 that an allocation of 60% stocks/40% bonds would keep risk below this level if we used the existing indexes of those two asset classes. This would have provided a return of 8.43% per year over the past 10 years (Table 3.2).

You may notice that the probabilities discussed do not match the probabilities that would be derived from a normal curve. We have used history to adjust the tails of the return distribution. In short, outliers (extreme values) exist. They shouldn't be assumed away.

With hardly any effort at all, you should be able to beat that return with the same level of risk. In fact, Tables 3.1 and 3.2 give examples of many allocations that would have done better using other indexes. But as discussed, selected portfolios in the various asset classes will usually outperform cap-weighted indexes.

Getting the Highest Return at a Given Risk Level

Once you have selected an appropriate level of risk, the next step is to create a portfolio that provides the highest return for that risk. Of course no one knows what the future holds, so the selection of individual assets must be based on your own estimates. But the information here should give you some idea of which classes and subclasses you should examine. In studying the data in Tables 3.3 and 3.4, remember that results for the past 10 years are somewhat different than over the past 50, and the last three years (2000–2002) have been very atypical. The correlations in Table 3.3 are close to those for the very long run even though there may be short-term variations.

How might you create your own portfolio? On paper, you will usually get the best return at a given risk level by combining the highest return asset class with the safest class in the proportion that gives you the desired risk level. For instance, looking at Tables 3.3 and 3.4, if this were 10 years ago, you could have selected a portfolio consisting of 90% REITs and 10% short-term bonds, maintained your RiskGrade at 58 and had a compound return of 9.7% a year. That combination also would have done well for the last three years.

It would have been hard to predict that result in advance, however, and asset class returns can change in a hurry. Even if you monitor your portfolio closely and adjust frequently, things can change too quickly to be invested in only one equity subclass. Remember how quickly energy stocks collapsed and tech stocks before that?

So how do you go about selecting which classes to be in? The first clue is the correlation between classes as shown in Table 3.3. The only negative correlations with the stock classes are in the bond classes. So to reduce risk significantly, there will need to be bond issues in your portfolio. The percentage you put in bonds depends on what else you choose.

In correlation Table 3.3 and risk-and-return Table 3.4, short-term bonds dominate long-term bonds in terms of their risk/reward trade-off. The small loss of return is well worth the larger reduction in risk. In fact, if your investment horizon is three years or longer, short-term government bonds have no risk. As explained in Chapter 2, there is no reason for individual investors to own long-term bonds in a balanced portfolio.

In selecting which other asset classes to invest in, look at those that have had the highest returns in the long run, with additional weight given to those also doing well in the short term. From the top classes look at the correlations and try to choose those with low correlations to each other. This is not a pure numbers game, nor is there one best way because the returns of each class for the future are not known.

With the standard deviations of each class and the correlation coefficients given in Tables 3.3 and 3.4, you can determine the standard deviation of any combination of asset classes in a portfolio. The standard deviation of the portfolio is a function of the standard deviations of each class, the fractional weight given each class and the correlations between each pair of classes. This is the same procedure as for individual assets. Further details are provided in Appendix A (A8).

Based on the preferences and biases of this book, the following is a more direct approach:

- Eliminate bonds, except for short-term bonds.

- Based on results from over the last 70 years, from this year, and from all long-term periods in between, eliminate all stocks on the S&P 500 index—along with any total stock market index fund (there are now some equally weighted indexes and these might be a possibility). If you are screening for individual stocks, you can simply eliminate stocks with over $2 billion market capitalization.

• The correlation between foreign and U.S. stocks is too great for there to be meaningful long-term diversification, and the loss of return is too great a price for such little short-term risk reduction. This eliminates foreign stocks.

• Toss out gold mining stocks, even though the correlations with other asset classes are low. The risk reduction effect is very short term and the long-term return reduction is severe. However, a small holding in mining stocks is not unreasonable.

• Eliminate small-cap growth stocks because of their performance and risk relative to small-cap value stocks, and their high correlation with micro-cap stocks.

• Categories not listed that may be suitable include mid-cap stocks. Mid-cap value stocks have a return similar to small-cap value. Also, you can include any value stock with a capitalization of less than $2 billion in your choices.

Beyond a bond portion, the suggested portfolio make up is REITs, small-cap and mid-cap value stocks, and micro-cap stocks. However, it would be wrong to suggest that equity investments in other categories are never successful. There are excellent investments in other categories; they are just not as common. Why look for gold in a well-worked mine when new veins exist elsewhere?

How do you define the stock size and style categories? There are no consensus definitions, but the Glossary at the back of this book provides recommendations.

One caution: When selecting value stocks, choose a real measure of value rather than the classification that splits all stocks into either growth or value. One criteria would be that the price-to-book ratio must be below 1.5, and lower, perhaps 1.0, is better.

In terms of the percentages to invest in each category, invest an approximately equal amount in each, and then after examining the risk of such a portfolio, invest enough in short-term bonds to reduce the risk level to one appropriate for you.

For example, an initial stock portion of the portfolio could be:

    25% micro cap (value or growth)
    25% small-cap value
    25% mid-cap value
    25% REITs

Remember from previous discussion that the best portfolio might come from only one or two of these classes.

How do you choose the specific investments

within each class? The methods of choosing a pool of potential stocks in each asset class have been the subject of thousands of books. You can design your own approach or you can rely on the advice of others. The process of diversifying the individual issues within each class was the subject of Chapter 2. The degree to which you are able to diversify and allocate among equity subclasses will reduce the percentage of low return, safe investments you will have to add to the portfolio to maintain your required risk level.

One effective approach, discussed in Chapter 2, is to select more stocks in an asset class than you actually want. You can then set up a correlation matrix based on historical prices and choose those with the lowest correlations with each other. Alternatively, you can enter the stocks into the RiskGrade tool on AAII's Web site and use the "what if" processes to find the lowest risk group. This was also illustrated in Chapter 2.

You should review the entire portfolio after you finish choosing individual investments in each class. Say you have four asset subclasses (not including your bond portfolio) and have selected 10 stocks in each of them. You can once again set up a correlation matrix or a RiskGrade portfolio and see if all of the individual issues are necessary. You may well find that many of the individual stocks are highly correlated even if they are in different subclasses and you can eliminate the ones you feel will produce the lowest returns.

If you prefer investing in mutual funds, there is no reason not to include funds that invest in the asset classes you need. However, as previously discussed, keep in mind that index funds and large-cap funds that are almost like index funds are ineffective. You can treat a fund just as a stock in setting up an effective portfolio and analyzing its risk. Some large-cap funds that use a different approach and are not "me too" funds might be included.

Once a suitable portfolio has been established, it is necessary to monitor and adjust it. With three or four equity asset subclasses, it will not be necessary to check risk levels constantly and, in fact, short-term variations should be ignored. If the risk of your portfolio starts to increase and continues to increase over a month or more, you should look at the components, see where the additional risk is coming from and make adjustments as necessary. While we are not discussing ways to choose stocks or asset classes, the approach used for doing this must also be monitored. Real estate, for example, has had long bull runs at times and even though it is an excellent hedge (low correlation) for other equities, REITs may not always have the returns reflected in Table 3.4. In fact, 1998 was a very poor year.

Monitoring can be done by looking at the components of your portfolio with the RiskGrades tool, or by looking at the risk levels of the mutual fund surrogates listed in Tables 3.3 and 3.4. The risk of the surrogate mutual funds can be found at Morningstar.com (see References) or other analytic sites.

Chapter

The Risk/Return Relationship

The introduction to this book laid out two basic principles that underlie any intelligent approach to investing. They are:

Basic Principle 1

Reduction in portfolio risk can be directly converted into increased return. There is no easier way to increase the return on a portfolio than to reduce its unnecessary risk.

Basic Principle 2

Any individual security should be selected not because it has the highest ratio of expected return to risk over your investment horizon, but rather because it increases the return-to-risk ratio of your entire portfolio more than any other security choice.

These principles are the foundation of the conviction that investing must have a portfolio orientation. The investment portfolio is more than the sum of its parts. The best overall returns for the individual investor may well come from a portfolio consisting of stocks with expected future returns lower than could have been selected. This chapter explains the importance of the portfolio approach and shows why it is better than simply going for the highest expected return stocks.

The Long-Term Impact of Lower Volatility

In Chapter 1, Table 1.1 illustrated that even though two assets may have equal arithmetic average returns, if one has a lower volatility (standard deviation), it will have a higher geometric average return and thus a higher terminal wealth. Table 4.1 goes a step further in this example.

Table 4.1: The Impact of Lower Volatili

	Period Return (%)					
	1	2	3	4	5	6
Portfolio A	10.0	10.0	10.0	10.0	10.0	10.0
Portfolio B	2.0	20.0	-6.0	28.0	-11.0	33.0

Terminal Wealth:

$$(1 + R_1)(1 + R_2)(1 + R_3)(1 + R_4)(1 + R_5)(1 + R_6)$$

Portfolio A:

$$(1.1)(1.1)(1.1)(1.1)(1.1)(1.1) = 1.77$$

Portfolio B:

$$(1.02)(1.20)(0.94)(1.28)(0.89)(1.33) = 1.74$$

As can be seen, Portfolio A with a lower average annual return has a higher geometric average return and terminal wealth than Portfolio B. This is due to the reduction in volatility (risk). Therefore, reducing risk directly increases the true rate of return (the geometric average).

Reducing Stock Risk Changes Asset Allocation

Chapter 3 illustrated that in order to maintain risk at an acceptable level for most investors, some quantity of bonds would have to be included in the portfolio's asset allocation (Table 3.1). This is

Arithmetic Average (%)	Geometric Average (%)	Standard Deviation (%)	Terminal Wealth* ($)
10.0	10.0	0.0	177,000
11.0	9.7	16.9	174,000

*$100,000 invested at the beginning of period 1.

because bonds are the only assets with very low or negative correlations to the various stock subclasses (Table 3.3). Because the return on bonds—particularly short-term bonds, which are most effective—is low compared to stock classes, there has to be a trade-off of return for risk reduction. It follows then that the lower the risk of the stock part of the portfolio, the lower the proportion of the portfolio that will have to be in bonds, and the higher the average return. Therefore, reducing the risk of the stock portion of the portfolio will directly translate into higher returns for the overall portfolio.

While this risk/return relationship is obviously true for typical investors who have some of their portfolio in low-return safe assets, it is also true for the aggressive investor. In the case of aggressive investors who are completely in stocks, reducing the risk of the stock portfolio would permit them to use margin (borrowing money to buy additional shares) and still maintain their desired level of risk. This would increase returns, assuming the returns are higher than the margin interest.

Effective diversification can reduce unnecessary risk, often with little effort. It should be apparent why Principle 1 is important to understand. An attitude of "find the best returns and risk will take care of itself" wastes the opportunity to increase returns.

The Trade-off of Return for Risk Reduction

When should you trade return for risk reduction? The ultimate opportunity is when you can no longer get rid of unnecessary risk and must accept the lower returns of safe bonds to bring your overall portfolio to the risk level you desire.

There are other times for trade-offs within the selection process of your stock portfolio. Since risk reduction can be converted to additional return, you are really looking at choices that involve accepting a lower return at one point to get a higher return at another. Table 4.1 illustrates the end product of this process. Assume the stocks in Portfolio A were chosen even though they had a lower expected return (10% versus 11%) than those in Portfolio B, and that these are historical results. A higher expected return was sacrificed when choosing the stocks in order to reduce portfolio risk. This choice translated into a gain in return that was higher than the expected return sacrificed.

What is the process by which this trade-off might occur? It follows the multiple asset model as shown in A8 in Appendix A; Table 4.2 illustrates a simple example using two stocks.

Table 4.2: The Risk/Return Trade-Off

	Expected Return (%)	Standard Deviation (%)	Return-to-Risk Ratio	Correlation With Stock A
Stock A	20.0	30.0	0.67	1.00
Stock B	18.0	20.0	0.90	0.70
Stock C	17.0	20.0	0.85	0.30
Portfolio AB	19.0	23.1	0.82	
Portfolio AC	18.5	20.4	0.90	

Assume you have purchased Stock A for your portfolio and must now choose between Stock B and Stock C. Stock B has a higher expected return. It also has a higher ratio of return to risk than Stock C, 0.90 (18%/20%) as opposed to 0.85 (17%/20%). Based on the return-to-risk ratio, you would choose Stock B if you were making a decision in isolation. But you want to see the impact of adding Stock B or Stock C to a portfolio containing Stock A.

The second half of Table 4.2 shows the returns and standard deviations for equally weighted portfolios AB and AC. The return-to-risk ratio is 0.90 for Portfolio AC and 0.82 for Portfolio AB. Therefore, Stock C is the better choice. This illustrates Principle 2.

Why does the higher return-to-risk ratio make it the better choice? If a standard deviation of 20.4% is your preferred risk level, you could buy Portfolio AC and have a return of 18.5%. To maintain a risk level of 20.4% while investing in Portfolio AB, you could only have 91% of your funds in this portfolio; the rest, 9%, would have to be in riskless securities returning an estimated 3.5%. This would result in a total return of 17.6% [(91% × 19%) + (9% × 3.5%)]—not as good as Portfolio AC at 18.5%.

Even if you wanted to accept more risk, you would receive a higher return by leveraging Portfolio AC with the use of margin to the level of risk you wanted. The overall return would be higher at any level of risk compared to investing in Portfolio AB. Why is this true? The lower correlation of Stock C with Stock A makes all the difference. And the impact of lower correlations becomes even stronger as the number of stocks involved increases.

You can now understand why all the media emphasis on specific stocks is distressing. When listening to experts answer questions about different stocks from callers on CNBC, you will sometimes hear them ask about the individual's risk situation, but you never hear anyone ask, "What other stocks are in your portfolio?" And, as this book has shown, that is the critical question.

This portfolio approach cannot be emphasized enough. If you were the manager or coach of a sports team, how do you decide which players to use in the game? The highest paid, the most famous, or the ones who will win more games and championships because of their contribution to the team's performance? Investing is a team sport and each individual security has to be measured not on some individual statistic, but on how it contributes to the portfolio's success.

No one knows for sure how any individual stock will perform, not even over the long run. But multiple stocks selected by rational criteria and then filtered through an analysis of how they interact with each other provides a portfolio that will, over any reasonable term, provide positive returns in excess of the returns of any of the popular indexes.

In an ideal long-term portfolio, it is likely that one or more assets will be performing poorly. This does not necessarily mean that they were poor choices. They may be providing diversification and be the superior performers when the economy changes in the next quarter.

Behavioral Finance

At various places, this book has alluded to problems with various assumptions of modern portfolio theory (MPT) and its underlying assumptions—rational investor behavior and the efficient market hypothesis (EMH). There is a growing body of evidence that:

1) The decreasing marginal utility of wealth is not the best explanation of observed risk aversion;

2) The behavior of individual and, in some cases, institutional investors is not rational in the accepted sense;

3) The market is less efficient than EMH postulates; and

4) Much of MPT rests on weak assumptions.

While it is not possible to go into all of this here, there are several books in the Bibliography (see Kahneman and also Shleifer) that do so very well. What is important to point out is that with the exception of the "outlier" problem when assuming a normal curve, the approaches in this book predate and do not depend on the core of MPT.

The "outlier" problem was discussed and that is why emphasis was given to looking at historical equity performance and adjusting for worst-case scenarios.

The one area of behavioral finance that is disturbing is the strong evidence that investors are less than rational in their decision making. Without strong determination, emotion will win over reason. All of the rules of efficient portfolio management will be useless if they are not followed.

Supplement for SSR Users

The *Stock Superstars Report* (*SSR*) is a portfolio-oriented, common stock advisory service. It is published by the American Association of Individual Investors (AAII) and delivered via Web site, E-mail, a telephone hotline, and print mailing. If you are not currently a subscriber, please log on to our Web site at www.stocksuperstars.com for a full description.

The purpose of this supplement is to help SSR subscribers integrate the concepts of this book with the use of the *SSR* service. To a great degree, the *SSR* emphasizes portfolio formation as well as individual stock selection and integrates these concepts following the principles described in Chapter 4. Consequently, *SSR* subscribers who purchase all 36 of the stocks in the recommended portfolio benefit from the risk reduction that has already been done.

However, subscribers who have decided to maintain a portfolio of fewer than the 36 stocks recommended should apply the principles of this book to their stock selection process. A minimum of 16 stocks is strongly advised and 20 to 24 is preferable—based on the risk-reducing impact of diversification. Holding 24 stocks will come close to the diversification effect of holding 36.

The basis for deciding how many stocks to hold relates to minimizing transaction costs. There are two components of transaction costs—commissions and the spread between the bid and ask price. These components operate in the opposite direction from each other. The greater the number of shares in each trade, the lower will be the commission as a percent of the acquisition or sale. On the other hand, if you are buying or selling a substantial amount of stock in a single trade, you will impact the spread and have to pay more for purchases and receive less for sales. You can work out the trade-off from experience and make your decision. In any event, hold at least 16 stocks and use a deep discount broker to minimize trading costs.

How do you decide which of the stocks to pick initially for your portfolio? And then, what process should you use to decide how to replace any stocks that are sold? The sections below provide some guidance.

First-Time Selection

First, and most important, divide the number of stocks across the *SSR* groupings as evenly as possible. This will eliminate much searching for low correlations. Within each category, it is generally best to choose the most recent recommendations because the criteria used for both return and risk selection is freshest. However, a few weeks is not going to make a great deal of difference on average.

Assume you decide on a portfolio of 16 stocks, four stocks from each group. You would take the most recent six recommendations from each group and analyze them for minimum risk. You can set up a correlation table as described, but it is much easier to use the analysis at the RiskGrades Web site. Put the six stocks from one group into a portfolio at RiskGrades.com with an equal dollar investment in each. Look at the risk impact of each stock and eliminate the stock with the highest risk contribution. Examine the portfolio again, look for the highest risk contribution, and then eliminate that stock. You are left with the four stocks with the best risk reduction possibilities in that group. If the risk contribution of all stocks is almost even, you can eliminate the oldest recommendations, or make your selections using other personal criteria. This procedure was illustrated in Chapter 2 (Figures 2.3 and 2.4 show the output from RiskGrades).

Ongoing Selection

When a stock you own is sold you must replace it. You can either replace the stock immediately or wait for the recommendation from *SSR*. You can choose a new stock from the recommended stocks that you don't own, including the most recent recommendation. Though the recommended stock is chosen by *SSR* with risk reduction in mind, it may not be the most efficient stock to add to your specific portfolio when you only own a subset of all recommended stocks. However, when examining the stocks you do not own for a replacement, be sure to choose one from the same group as the recommended stock.

Keep your actual portfolio on RiskGrades.com. After eliminating the stock sold, check all the unowned stocks in the group to see which, when combined with your existing portfolio, will give the lowest portfolio RiskGrade. There is a "what if" function to make this easier. Use the dollar amount that you will actually invest in a new stock to determine the number of shares assigned to the stocks you are evaluating.

The above procedures should enable you to achieve almost all of the benefits of the *SSR* approach even if you have fewer stocks. Again, 16 stocks is the recommended minimum; move to 20 as soon as practical.

Appendix A

A1: Arithmetic Average, Geometric Average, and Terminal Wealth

The arithmetic average is what we generally think of as the average. It can be calculated in Excel using the AVERAGE function. The formula for the average (mean) return from a series of returns is:

$$r_{AA} = \frac{1}{n} \sum_{i=1}^{n} r_i = [r_1 + r_2 ... r_n] \div n$$

where r_i = return for period i

The geometric average (mean) is reduced relative to the arithmetic average as a function of volatility. It can be calculated in Excel using the GEOMEAN function. The formula for geometric average is:

$$r_{GA} = \sqrt[n]{(1 + r_1)(1 + r_2)...(1 + r_n)} - 1$$

where r_i = return for period i

Terminal wealth is determined by the geometric average. It can be calculated by using the GEOMEAN function of Excel, adding 1 and then raising it to the nth power. The formula for terminal wealth is:

$$\text{Terminal Wealth} = (1 + r_{GA})^n$$

or

$$\text{Terminal Wealth} = (1 + r_1)(1 + r_2)...(1 + r_n)$$

In the range of returns most commonly used the following approximation is useful:

$$\text{Geometric Average Return} = \text{Arithmetic Average Return} - \frac{\text{Standard Deviation}^2}{2}$$

Using numbers from Table 4.1 (Portfolio B) on pages 62-63:

$$= \quad 0.110 \quad - \quad \frac{0.169^2}{2}$$

$$= \quad 0.110 \quad - \quad \frac{0.029}{2}$$

$$= \quad 0.110 \quad - \quad 0.015$$

$$= \quad 0.095 \text{ or } 9.5\%$$

A2: Standard Deviation

Standard deviation is calculated as the square root of the average of the deviations from the arithmetic average, squared. The standard deviation of a security's rates of return has the formula:

$$\sigma = \sqrt{\frac{\sum_{i=1}^{n}\left(r_i - r_{AA}\right)^2}{n}}$$

r_i = return for period i

r_{AA} = arithmetic average return

To calculate standard deviation using Excel, use the STDEV function. The Yahoo! Web site (finance.yahoo.com) can be used to obtain necessary data. Get an extended quote for any security or mutual fund. Choose historical prices. Set up for month-end prices if using two or more years. Set up for weekly prices if using one year or less. Choose download, and prices will be placed in an Excel spreadsheet in column A. These are prices, not returns, so in cell B2 enter "=A2/A1 – 1" and then drag down the B column. You can then use the B column in the STDEV formula. The standard deviation must be adjusted to put it in the usual annual form. If you used monthly data, multiply by 3.464; if weekly data was used, multiply by 7.21. These figures are the square root of the number of periods in a year.

A3: Skewness

Skewness is the tendency for a distribution curve to be stretched out more on one side (asymmetrical), as shown below. The skewness can be in either direction, but in security returns the tail would be to the right. When the lognormal curve is used, skewness becomes slight.

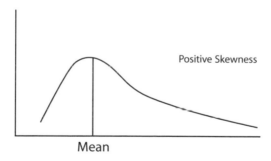

Positive Skewness

Mean

A4: Peakedness (Kurtosis)

This is a measure of how peaked a distribution is beyond that of a normal curve. Security returns are peaked as illustrated:

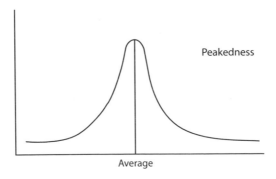

Peakedness

Average

A5: Normal Distribution Curve

The normal distribution curve, as illustrated, can be described by only two measures, mean and standard deviation. We know the percentage of the distribution that is within any number of standard deviations.

- 68% of returns fall within one standard deviation on each side of the average. There's a 32% chance of returns falling outside this range and a 16% chance of returns falling on any one side.

- 95% of returns fall within two standard deviations on each side of the average. There's a 5% chance of returns falling outside this range and a 2.5% chance of returns falling on any one side.

- 99.7% of returns fall within three standard deviations on each side of the average. There's a 0.3% chance of returns falling outside this range and a 0.15% chance of returns falling on any one side.

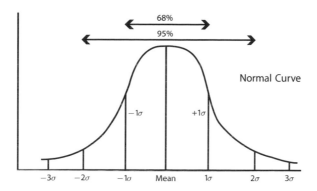

A6: Semi-Variance

Semi-variance is a measure of volatility that only measures returns below the average. While it makes intuitive sense, results will be very close to variance (variance is standard deviation squared) and the semi–standard deviation will be very close on a relative basis to standard deviation. The formula is the same as in A2, but only uses the returns (r) below the average (r_{AA}) and n is the number of returns used.

$$\sigma = \sqrt{\frac{\sum_{i=1}^{n}\left(r_i - r_{AA}\right)^2}{n}}$$

r_i = return for period i
r_{AA} = arithmetic average return
where ($r_i - r_{AA}$) for all $r_i \leq 0$

77

A7: Beta

Beta, as generally used, is the slope of the regression line between the returns over time of an individual security and an index of the entire market. The formula is:

$$B = \frac{\mathrm{cov}(r_m, r_s)}{\mathrm{var}\,m} = \frac{\sum_{i=1}^{n}(r_{mi} - r_{ma})(r_{si} - r_{sa})}{\sigma_m^2}$$

r_{mi} = market rates of return

r_{si} = security rates of return

r_{ma}, r_{sa} = arithmetic average of the market return and security return

A8: Standard Deviation of a Portfolio

The portfolio standard deviation can be determined most easily by using the period rates of return of the portfolio and applying the regular standard deviation formula (A2). However, there may not be a history of portfolio returns. In that case, the standard deviation of the portfolio can be determined by the standard deviations of the individual securities, the correlations between them, and the weight of each security in the portfolio, using the following formula:

$$\sigma_{port} = \sum_{i=1}^{n} w_i^2 \sigma_i^2 + \sum_{i=1}^{n}\sum_{j=1}^{n} w_i w_j r_{ij} \sigma_i \sigma_j$$

w_i = proportion of portfolio in asset i

r_{ij} = coefficient of correlation i, j

The calculations are quite extensive if many securities are involved. A more practical way of carrying out such an analysis would be to follow the spreadsheet procedure outlined in A2 for calculating the standard deviation of one security. As described in A2, download the historical prices into Excel from Yahoo! and calculate the returns for each period from the prices. Do the same for each security and then put columns with the return data for each stock in adjacent columns. Create a new column that is the average of the returns for each period. Then use STDEV to calculate the standard deviation for the portfolio. Remember to convert to an annual basis, as in A2. If the securities have different weights, the average column should be a weighted average. This can be accomplished by weighting each return with the proportion of dollars in each asset. The sum of the weights must equal 1.0.

Appendix B

How do you set a suitable risk level for yourself? One way is to establish a worst-case scenario—the percentage loss that would occur if diversification failed and all of your assets went down simultaneously.

Your own risk level is whatever percentage loss you could withstand without abandoning your portfolio positions. In an article that appeared in the AAII Journal, *John Markese discussed the approach in the context of mutual fund investing, and it is reprinted here. This approach could easily be adapted for those building their own portfolio.*

Financial Check-Up: Figuring Out Your Mutual Fund Portfolio*

By John Markese, President of AAII

Here is an approach and a simple worksheet that will help you get a grip around all your funds as a portfolio. It will give you insights into your funds individually and force you to assess whether the funds you own make sense when they are taken together as a portfolio.

The Framework

The worksheet in Table 1 provides you with a framework to evaluate expected risk and return for individual funds and your portfolio of funds.

---

*This article originally appeared in the August 2001 issue of the AAII Journal.

Table 1: Worksheet for Mutual Fund Portfolios

Fund Category	A Portfolio Weight (%)	B Annual Yield* (%)	C Annual Capital Gain* (%)	D Downside Risk** (%)
Money Market	____	4	0	0
Bond, General	____	6	0	10
Corporate	____	6	0	10
Government	____	5	0	10
High-Yield Corporate	____	10	0	20
Stock, General	____	1	10	30
Large Stock	____	2	8	30
Small Stock	____	0	12	40
Growth Stock	____	0	11	40
Value Stock	____	3	8	20
Sector	____	0 to 6	4 to 14	20 to 70
International	____	2	10	40
Emerging Markets	____	0	14	70
Total	100%			

Average Portfolio Yield	=	Add A x B for each fund category
Average Portfolio Capital Gain	=	Add A x C for each fund category
Total Return	=	Average yield plus average capital gain
Downside Risk	=	Add A x D for each specific fund category

*Long-term average annual compound yield and capital gains estimates assume reinvestments of income; significant annual variation can be expected for categories and individual funds.
**Annual decline potential based on severe bear market conditions and the conservative assumption that all fund categories would decline simultaneously.

There are some assumptions built into this approach that are important. First, the annual yield and annual capital gains percentages for the fund categories are long-term averages that can vary year-to-year but are historically reasonable. The longer your investment period, the more likely you are to experience similar returns.

Can your individual fund performances differ from these averages? Yes—and the differences can be significant. The more diversified your fund, however, the more likely that it will be similar to the average. However, the more funds trade securities, incurring transaction costs, and the greater the expense ratio, the more likely that funds will underperform these numbers. And it is important to note that these returns are before taxes, so the less tax-efficient your fund is, the lower your aftertax returns will be.

In other words, index funds will be closer to these long-term averages, and actively managed individual funds will have performance distributed both above and below these numbers. But it is important to remember that these are only informed guesses, and future performance may well differ from history and will certainly do so in the short run. If you feel the need to adjust any of these figures, particularly the stock fund numbers, err on the conservative side, reducing the capital gains component. These numbers would probably be 1% to 2% lower if the experience of the last decade were completely removed. Also, dividend yields have dropped dramatically over the same period, and these expected annual yield figures are near all-time lows. And if your mutual fund is not an index fund with naturally low expenses (expenses are netted out against income) the yields will be even lower.

Risk: The Downside

The downside risk measure is a practical look at what might happen to the value of your mutual fund portfolio in a worst-case scenario.

What is a worst-case? That would occur if
diversification among different fund categories
fails and all of your funds fall in unison. The
downside percentage loss in value in any one year
for the mutual fund categories is based on post–
World War II experiences for average funds. Are
there plenty of funds that have done worse in any
year? Yes, but they again tend to deviate
significantly from these norms when they are not
as broadly diversified as the category average.

Taking a look at the amount by which your
mutual fund portfolio could drop in a year will
give you a feeling for just how appropriate your
fund portfolio risk level is relative to your risk
tolerance. Converting the percentage downside
potential of the funds to dollars, which will be
explained, is the test of your ability to sustain
short-term losses without breaking your long-
term financial plan (selling off investments at
absolutely the wrong time, after a market drop).

Fund categories are listed in the worksheet, and
general entries are made for money market, bond,
and stock funds. Under the bond and stock fund
general categories, there are breakdowns of fund
types that cover almost all funds.

Municipal bond funds are not a separate listing,
but adjusting yields for long-term government
bond funds or money market funds for taxes
(1.00 minus your federal tax rate in decimal form
times the government bond or money market
yield) will give you a useful approximation.

Money market funds and short-term
government bond funds have yields that are close

enough for planning purposes, and the yields on intermediate bond funds are equally close to long-term bond funds. Capital gains for money market funds are zero because of their structure. Capital gains for bond funds are shown to be zero under the assumption that over the long-term, the impact of interest rate charges and economic cycles will net out capital gains and losses to zero. Clearly, actual holding periods, particularly short-term ones, could produce significant capital gains or losses—primarily for long-term bond funds with average maturities of bonds in the portfolio over 10 years.

Under the stock category, both stock size— large and small—and investment approach— growth and value—are separately listed.

Small stocks are riskier than large stocks, and a growth approach is riskier than a value approach. But the surprise is that value stocks tend to have about the same returns in the long run as growth stocks, although the growth approach beat value for most of the last decade of the last century. Probably the highest historical returns, but not the highest risk, have been in portfolios holding small value stocks. If you are not quite certain where a stock fund fits, but you are sure it is diversified, just think of the general stock category as an appropriate match. And if you have a balanced fund, one that holds both stocks and bonds, 50% in each for example, half would be general bond and half general stock.

Sector funds are all over the board as the name indicates, but only very concentrated, high-risk funds, such as in technology or biotechnology, would approach a 14% long-term capital gain average and then it would be paired with a 0% yield. An average utility stock sector fund might be close to a 4% yield and a 6% capital gain, as an illustration of how to use the sector figures. The downside risk for the biotech fund or technology sector fund is 70%, for the utility, 20%. The higher the yield, the lower the capital gains, and the less the downside risk; conversely, the lower the yield, the higher the capital gains, and the greater the downside risk.

International stock funds are affected by currency exchange risk and are inherently riskier, even when investing in large international companies that are indistinguishable from large domestic companies. Emerging market funds, however, have greater currency risks but also significant risk from government instability and less diversified economies. Funds that hold stock from many emerging markets are clearly less risky than single-country or regional emerging market funds.

How It Works

Time for an example. Example 1 shows how you can use the worksheet by plugging in your mutual fund portfolio and doing some simple arithmetic. The portfolio weight percentage is the market value of a fund divided by the total market value of all funds in your portfolio. If you have financial investments other than mutual funds and want to use this approach for your entire portfolio, take the market value of each investment—stock, bond, or fund—and divide it by the total market value of all financial

Example 1: An Aggressive Portfolio

Fund Category	Portfolio Weight (%)	Annual Yield (%)	Annual Capital Gain (%)	Downside Risk (%)
Money Market	10	4	0	0
Bond, General	___	6	0	10
Corporate	___	6	0	10
Government	___	5	0	10
High-Yield Corporate	___	10	0	20
Stock, General	___	1	10	30
Large Stock	30	2	8	30
Small Stock	30	0	12	40
Growth Stock	___	0	11	40
Value Stock	___	3	8	20
Sector	___	0 to 6	4 to 14	20 to 70
International	25	2	10	40
Emerging Markets	5	0	14	70
Total	100%			

Average Portfolio Yield = 1.5% = $(0.10 \times 4) + (0.30 \times 2) + (0.30 \times 0) + (0.25 \times 2) + (0.05 \times 0)$

Average Portfolio Capital Gain = 9.2% = $(0.10 \times 0) + (0.30 \times 8) + (0.30 \times 12) + (0.25 \times 10) + (0.05 \times 14)$

Total Return = 10.7% = 1.50% + 9.20%

Downside Risk = 34.5% = $(0.10 \times 0) + (0.30 \times 30) + (0.30 \times 40) + (0.25 \times 40) + (0.05 \times 70)$

investments. Then fit your non-fund investments into an appropriate category. Here, the example assumes only mutual fund investments and represents an aggressive portfolio mix appropriate for investors with long horizons, low cash needs, and a strong tolerance for short-term downside moves in their total portfolio.

In Example 1, yield is relatively low, at 1.5%, and it should be reinvested if income is not required. Mutual fund shares, however, can always be redeemed to provide cash, and importantly, long-term capital gains are taxed at

Example 2: A Conservative Portfolio

Fund Category	Portfolio Weight (%)	Annual Yield (%)	Annual Capital Gain (%)	Downside Risk (%)
Money Market	10	4	0	0
Bond, General	___	6	0	10
Corporate	___	6	0	10
Government	30	5	0	10
High-Yield Corporate	10	10	0	20
Stock, General	___	1	10	30
Large Stock	___	2	8	30
Small Stock	___	0	12	40
Growth Stock	___	0	11	40
Value Stock	40	3	8	20
Sector (Utility)	10	4	6	20
International	___	2	10	40
Emerging Markets	___	0	14	70
Total	100%			

Average Portfolio Yield = 4.5% = $(0.10 \times 4) + (0.30 \times 5) + (0.10 \times 10) + (0.40 \times 3) + (0.10 \times 4)$

Average Portfolio Capital Gain = 3.8% = $(0.10 \times 0) + (0.30 \times 0) + (0.10 \times 0) + (0.40 \times 8) + (0.10 \times 6)$

Total Return = 8.3% = 4.5% + 3.8%

Downside Risk = 15.0% = $(0.10 \times 0) + (0.30 \times 10) + (0.10 \times 20) + (0.40 \times 20) + (0.10 \times 20)$

lower rates than dividend income. The capital gains, at 9.2%, are substantial, and compounded over long periods will create substantial wealth. The short-term cost of this long-term wealth accumulation is portfolio volatility—this aggressive portfolio may decline by more than one-third (34.5%) in value in a single year. That means that if you have $1 million invested, you may have a potential unrealized loss of $345,000. The question you must ask is whether you can sustain this kind of loss without breaking your long-term plan. If not, reduce the total commitment to stocks across the board, eliminate high-risk investments such as emerging markets, and increase investments in money market funds, or bond funds with shorter average maturities.

At the other extreme is Example 2, a very conservative portfolio, perhaps for someone in retirement. The stock/fixed-income breakdown is 50%/50%, and the stock fund portion is decidedly income-oriented. The 40% in value stock funds could conceivably be in an index fund, in separate large-cap and small-cap funds, one broadly diversified value fund, or some combination. The 10% in a utility sector fund would be somewhat redundant if the value funds had significant positions in utility stocks.

The bond portion of the portfolio is primarily in a government bond fund. An average maturity for this fund in the seven- to 10-year range would capture almost all the return of the longer maturity bonds while avoiding some of the volatility of the longest sector of the yield curve. The 10% in the corporate high-yield (junk) category is a pure income boost supported by a diversified holding in junk bonds, which spreads default risk over a large portfolio base. And while the downside of the high-yield category is double that of the government bond fund category, it is still less than the growth stock category.

Notice in Example 2, as compared to the aggressive portfolio in Example 1, that yield (income) is up, capital gains are down, and total return is down. But downside risk is more than halved, at 15% for this portfolio. The trade-off: lower return for higher income, and lower growth for lower risk.

Note, however, that if the stock component drops much below 50%, the growth—capital gains—that can be generated by this portfolio starts to fall below most expectations of the long-term inflation rate experience of 3% to 4%, eroding the real value of the portfolio over time. The capital gains rate for this conservative portfolio falls within the long-term inflation range by generating a 3.8% growth rate.

Running the Numbers

The worksheet is designed to "put up" your portfolio and see what it may generate over time in terms of income, return, and risk. It also allows you to move the mix around and observe the trade-offs. When you multiply the downside percentage against your portfolio value, you can test your financial courage.

A side benefit of running your portfolio through this worksheet is that it forces you to categorize your investments, and to evaluate whether your portfolio is redundant, has gaps, is concentrated, diversified, rational versus your goals, or just a big cumulative, historical mess.

And while you're at it, count the number of funds you have. If the number of fund choices under your control (not in 401(k) or 403(b) plans) is out of control (eight is typically enough), it's probably time to clean house.

Glossary

arithmetic average: see A1 in Appendix A.

asset allocation: the distribution of investment funds among distinct classes of assets, such as stocks, bonds and real estate.

beta: a measure of a stock's risk relative to the market, usually the Standard & Poor's 500 index. The market's beta is always 1.0; a beta higher than 1.0 indicates that, on average, when the market rises, the stock will rise to a greater extent and when the market falls, the stock will fall to a greater extent. A beta lower than 1.0 indicates that, on average, the stock will move to a lesser extent than the market. The higher the beta, the greater the risk. (See A7 in Appendix A.)

capitalization-weighted: weighting the holdings of a fund or index based on market capitalizations (larger companies take a larger position in the portfolio).

correlation: the relationship between two assets. Correlation coefficients are used to measure how closely a pair of asset classes tends to move in relation to each other. A perfect positive correlation of 1.0 indicates identical fluctuations—both classes tend to move up and down at the same time by similar amounts. The lower the correlation, the better the diversification; −1.0 means perfect negative correlation.

diversification: the process of accumulating

securities in different investments, types of industries, risk categories, and companies in order to reduce the potential harm of loss from any one investment.

geometric average: see A1 in Appendix A.

growth stocks: stocks of companies with rapid and expanding growth.

index fund: a mutual fund whose portfolio is designed to track a particular market index.

junk bond: bond purchased for speculative purposes; usually rated BB and lower and has a high default risk.

large-cap stocks: stocks with market capitalizations over $2 billion.

long-term bonds: bonds with a weighted-average maturity of greater than 10 years. The longer the maturity, the greater the change in value when interest rates change. Longer-term bonds are riskier than shorter-term bonds and they usually offer higher yields.

market capitalization: number of common stock shares outstanding times share price. Provides a measure of firm size.

micro-cap stocks: stocks with market capitalizations under $150 million.

mid-cap stocks: stocks with market capitalizations between $500 million and $2 billion.

REIT: real estate investment trust; similar to mutual funds except they invest in real estate enterprises, primarily the ownership, renting and managing of properties.

return-to-risk ratio: return of a security or portfolio divided by its risk (standard deviation).

risk: possibility that an investment's actual return will be different than expected; includes the possibility of losing some or all of the original investment. Measured by variability of historical returns or dispersion of historical returns around their average return.

RiskGrade: a measure that standardizes risk by taking the average standard deviation of all the world's equities and assigning it a standard deviation value of 100. All other standard deviations are expressed as a percentage of that figure. Developed by RiskMetrics Group: see www.riskgrades.com.

S&P 500 index: broad-based index based on the average performance of approximately 500 widely held common stocks and market-cap weighted.

semi-variance: see A6 in Appendix A.

short-term bonds: bonds with a weighted-average maturity of less than three years.

skewness: see A3 in Appendix A.

small-cap stocks: stocks with market capitalizations of $500 million or less.

standard deviation: a measure of the degree to which returns of an asset vary around the mean. (See A2 in Appendix A.)

systematic risk: the volatility all securities face that cannot be diversified away; market risk. Alternatively, the volatility due to a security's unique characteristics is unsystematic risk, which can be reduced by combining the security with other dissimilar securities.

value stocks: stocks of companies whose price looks cheap relative to earnings, assets, dividends or cash flow.

Wilshire 5000 index: a broad-based, cap-weighted index of stocks. Includes virtually all liquid securities (about 7,000).

Bibliography & References

Books and Articles

AAII's Individual Investor's Shadow Stock Portfolio (formerly called the Beginner's Portfolio): This is a real portfolio that for 10 years has followed a simple process of investing in micro-cap value stocks with a management approach requiring a minimum amount of time. It has been used to experiment and provide insight into methods of practical stock portfolio management. For the past 10 years, its compound rate of return, after all costs, was 13.3% with a standard deviation below that of the S&P 500. For further explanation of the Individual Investor's Shadow Stock Portfolio, see "The AAII Beginner's Portfolio: An Annual Performance Review," April 2003 *AAII Journal*; available on AAII.com. It includes a 10-year summary.

Bernstein, Peter L., "Against the Gods: The Remarkable Story of Risk," John Wiley & Sons, 1998. Interesting book about the development of the concepts of risk. Understandable coverage of prospect theory and chaos theory, both of which challenge conventional theories of risk.

Bernstein, Peter L., editor, "The Portable MBA in Investment," John Wiley & Sons, 1995. Very succinct coverage of investment theory with all the formulae. Requires knowledge of statistics, but can be read for the concepts and the math

95

glossed over. Excellent as a reference.

Brinson, Gary, L., Randolph Hood, and Gilbert Beebower, "Determinants of Portfolio Performance," Financial Analysts Journal, May-June 1991. This is the work that led to emphasis on asset allocation, but has been misunderstood.

Fama, Eugene F., "The Behavior of Stock Market Prices," Journal of Business, January 1965. Early work showing that stock returns are not normally distributed, likely with infinite variance.

Fama, Eugene F. and Kenneth French, "The Cross-Section of Expected Stock Returns," Journal of Finance, June 1992. This article contains two interesting aspects. First, it supports the growing disillusion with beta as a useful measure. Second, and more importantly, it provides extensive research support for two anomalies in efficient market theory. Small-capitalization stocks provide higher returns than large-capitalization stocks, and the smaller the better. And high value stocks (measured by low price-to-book ratios) provide higher returns than low value stocks, and the greater the value the better.

Kahneman, Daniel and Amos Tversky, "Prospect Theory: An Analysis of Decision Making Under Risk," Economterica, No. 2, 1979. Early work showing that decision-making is often not rational by traditional measures.

Lowenstein, Roger, "When Genius Failed: The Rise and Fall of Long-Term Capital Management," Random House, 2000. The story of the failure of LTCM and the contribution of modern portfolio theory to the collapse.

Malkiel, Burton G., "A Random Walk Down Wall Street," Norton, 1999. Classic book covering all aspects of modern portfolio theory, including criticisms. Very enjoyable reading.

Mandelbrot, Benoit, "The Variations of Certain Speculative Prices," Journal of Business, October, 1963. Early work showing stock prices are not normally distributed.

McMillan, Lawrence G., "Options as a Strategic Investment, 4th Edition," Prentice Hall Press, 2001. Very complete coverage of option theory and practice.

Shleifer, Andrei, "Inefficient Markets: An Introduction to Behavioral Finance," Oxford University Press, 2000. Discussion of problems with the efficient market hypothesis from an economist's viewpoint.

Stock Superstars Report. A portfolio-oriented stock advisory service published by AAII. See www.stocksuperstars.com for details.

Web Sites

American Association of Individual Investors (AAII)
www.aaii.com
Financial information and resources.

Morningstar.com
www.morningstar.com

97

Extensive information on mutual funds including historical risk and return information.

NAREIT
www.nareit.com
Web site of the National Association of Real Estate Investment Trusts. Provides list of REITs and statistical information.

R

w
o   on and historical data on

www.riskgrades.com
Provides extensive information and analysis of stocks and portfolios with emphasis on risk characteristics and risk/return relationships.

Stock Superstars Report
www.stocksuperstars.com
AAII's stock portfolio advisory service.

Wilshire
www.wilshire.com
Source of information and historical data on all the indexes maintained by Wilshire. Source of unweighted indexes and specialty indexes.

Yahoo! Finance
finance.yahoo.com
Resource for a variety of financial information. Extended stock and mutual fund quotes provide price history that can be downloaded into Excel for statistical analysis.

of the failure of LTCM and the contribution of modern portfolio theory to the collapse.

Malkiel, Burton G., "A Random Walk Down Wall Street," Norton, 1999. Classic book covering all aspects of modern portfolio theory, including criticisms. Very enjoyable reading.

Mandelbrot, Benoit, "The Variations of Certain Speculative Prices," Journal of Business, October, 1963. Early work showing stock prices are not normally distributed.

McMillan, Lawrence G., "Options as a Strategic Investment, 4th Edition," Prentice Hall Press, 2001. Very complete coverage of option theory and practice.

Shleifer, Andrei, "Inefficient Markets: An Introduction to Behavioral Finance," Oxford University Press, 2000. Discussion of problems with the efficient market hypothesis from an economist's viewpoint.

Stock Superstars Report. A portfolio-oriented stock advisory service published by AAII. See www.stocksuperstars.com for details.

Web Sites

American Association of Individual Investors (AAII)
www.aaii.com
Financial information and resources.

Morningstar.com
www.morningstar.com

Extensive information on mutual funds including historical risk and return information.

NAREIT
www.nareit.com
Web site of the National Association of Real Estate Investment Trusts. Provides list of REITs and statistical information.

Reis
www.reis.com
Offers detailed information and historical data on REITs.

RiskGrades
www.riskgrades.com
Provides extensive information and analysis of stocks and portfolios with emphasis on risk characteristics and risk/return relationships.

Stock Superstars Report
www.stocksuperstars.com
AAII's stock portfolio advisory service.

Wilshire
www.wilshire.com
Source of information and historical data on all the indexes maintained by Wilshire. Source of unweighted indexes and specialty indexes.

Yahoo! Finance
finance.yahoo.com
Resource for a variety of financial information. Extended stock and mutual fund quotes provide price history that can be downloaded into Excel for statistical analysis.